Beginning with
an empty page

PETER YELDHAM

Beginning with an empty page

Published by Peter Yeldham
34A Jamieson Parade, Collaroy 2097
© 2020 Peter Yeldham
Produced by Bobby Graham Publishers
www.bgpublishers.com.au

All rights reserved

Cover and book design by Elise Knotek, Stripe Design
Digital editions produced by SunTecIndia
www.suntecindia.com
Printed by Ingram Spark
www.ingramspark.com

First edition 2020

ISBN 978-0-6486686-5-7 (print)
ISBN 978-0-6486686-6-4 (digital)

CONTENTS

Prologue	vii
Part One: Early Years	1
Part Two: Love and a Library	19
Part Three: Radio Days	28
Part Four: England	38
Part Five: The Sixties	55
Part Six: After the Oaks	112
Part Seven: Returning	118
Part Eight: Cook and the ABC	134
Part Nine: What's a Computer?	144
Part Ten: Lonely Years	179
Part Eleven: Wollstonecraft	187
Part Twelve: Interviews and Afterthoughts	200
Part Thirteen: Emails, Diaries, Letters and Selected Works	210

PROLOGUE

I find the first page of a new book is often confronting. It sometimes takes days until I'm satisfied with the first page, and comfortable with the main characters. After that I can still spend hours over their appearances and names.

I also find titles challenging. An alternate title for this book came after meeting an actor friend for lunch, and waiting while he signed autographs for a queue of fans. Writers rarely received this recognition, so it was a surprise, when two young girls were left, and one came to ask me to sign my autograph. As they walked away I heard her friend ask, 'Who was that?' 'Not a clue' she said, *'but he might be someone.'*

*****

From the age of twelve I wanted to be a writer. This was dismissed by my family as signs of early lunacy. My father said I should get a secure job, and write, *if I must*, at night. That would be sensible, he said. In my teens I was constantly advised about being sensible.

These were arid years when the word 'writer' was a more popular term for a naval clerk. A mention of how I tried to earn a living brought the predictable reply…*in the navy are you, sport?* It was a time when there was no Australia Council or Literary Fellowships, when films were only made with Hollywood stars, and local actors had supporting roles. Novelists were few, Australian playwrights an almost unknown species. In this bleak era I had just one believer—my maternal grandmother who bought me a dictionary as encouragement. I had another supporter when I met my wife. At the time she had full employment as a secretary while I was taking various part-time jobs to survive. It was on our second Christmas eve, her twenty-second birthday that she insisted I give up dead-end jobs and stay home to write, as she believed that it was our future, and until then she'd be the breadwinner for as long as it took. This is a personal story that began with trying to be a writer in a very different Australia. It is also a tribute to my wife who believed most things were possible, and helped to make dreams come true.

*****

PART ONE: EARLY YEARS

I only knew my mother from photographs, for she died when I was two years old. The family album showed her nursing me or my twin brothers in their first months, a slim attractive woman with a radiant smile. She was only twenty nine; it was shockingly unexpected, having a huge effect on our lives, and not one for the better.

In time I learnt more about her. She was born in New York, and when the family came to Sydney she was educated at Abbotsleigh. In her final year she was the Senior Prefect, and after her death there was annual prize awarded in her memory. She met my father when both their families had summer holidays at Collaroy. He was a medical student, and after their marriage they moved to Gladstone on the New South Wales coast, where he became the local doctor. From the photos it is clear the time in Gladstone was happy. Later in my life everyone had stories of that time, like our uncle, a survivor from the 1914 war with a tin leg, who allowed my brothers and me to beat a drumstick on it, while his sister played the violin. I heard about the house parties and influx of friends, as well as visits of grandparents and doting Aunts and Uncles. Sadly I remember none of this until life changed, when we moved to Lakemba in Sydney. Our father bought a new medical practice there, owned by a friend of his. The friend had an unmarried sister, and that was how we acquired a stepmother.

My first recollection of childhood was an insistence that we must call her "mother." I'm told she declared her ability to look after the three of us, but almost immediately we had a resident nurse. During the next ten years there was a steady succession of them. They fed and supervised us in our *quarters*, which was a segregated area at the back of the new house where we now lived, and where our step-mother and father came to say a brief goodnight when we'd been put to bed.

It seemed at variance to the life I'd known; no hugs, no warmth, no loving words. We were confined to this sector with its own bathroom and kitchen, as well as a living room where our meals were shared with the nurse. There was a combined bedroom for the twins, and a partitioned cubicle served as a bedroom for me. We spent our youth in this enclave, and the rest of the house was divided as securely as the Berlin Wall.

A swing door in the hallway served as the partition, and beyond it we were not welcome. My father's surgery was in the front of the house, a region my brothers and I could only visit if we needed a vaccination or had a minor illness. To this day I can recollect how it always felt like two quite different homes; one was ours, the other, securely beyond the swing door was theirs.

I never learned to accept or understand it. Even writing this so long afterwards, it seems unreal to me. As we grew older and had school friends, we avoided inviting them home; we were embarrassed to have anyone know the peculiar segregated kind of life we led. Unwilling to put up with this domestic apartheid was one of the reasons why, when I felt old enough to revolt, I moved out. But that was after a long and unhappy childhood.

In those early days I was led to believe this way of life was normal, but each month it felt more desperate. It was perplexing not seeing our relatives, in particular my maternal grandmother. Her visits had been an important part of my life; I was her first grandchild, and doubtless spoilt, but I felt a loss, unable to understand her absence. Meanwhile I had to obey orders and defer to our father's wife as our mother. It was only when we grew older that my brothers and I found a label to use in private. Her first name was Elfie, so we secretly called her the Elf. *To avoid a tedious repetition of the term step-mother, she is the Elf from now on.*

I was six when she persuaded my father I should go to boarding school. By then the family affiliations of Gladstone were fractured. She tolerated us seeing our father's parents for a brief visit, but her antipathy was reserved for our maternal grandmother, my favourite relative who I'd christened 'Bah.' It was a name my infant tongue had found easier to say than grandma, becoming a name that was adopted by all our future cousins, and one we still use to this day, when speaking of her. I asked my dad if I could see her before leaving for boarding school. He said "ask your mother," but, as expected, the answer was an evasive "no".

The school was in the Blue Mountains. I was the youngest there, I remember that. I was homesick, missing my twin brothers who were now four years old. I also remember being terrified at night, for the toilet block seemed about a hundred metres distance from the dormitories, and an urgent call of nature meant running through the dark, fearful of spider webs and snakes. At the age of six my imagination could move much faster than my legs.

I waited for promised letters from Bah, but there were none. This baffled me, making me feel I'd been abandoned, unaware that for weeks she wrote letters I never saw, and she was meanwhile wondering if I'd forgotten my promise to write in reply. After some months she decided the only way to find out was to drive to the mountains, and take me for a picnic. There was a furore when she arrived. The headmaster told her he was under instruction to forbid any contact, and asked her to leave. She also learned all her letters had been diverted to Lakemba by request. Only letters with the home address were allowed, he explained, not liking the situation but having no option.

In the end, after she pointed out how far she'd come, and how unfair it was, the headmaster apparently relented. He permitted us to meet, but only in the school grounds. The picnic she'd planned at the Three Sisters in Katoomba with its scenic railway was forbidden; it had to take place in front of the school sports pavilion, where various kids came to stare and comment about what was going on. She tried to explain that she couldn't come again; it would only cause trouble, and she hoped to eventually make peace with my step-mother, so my brothers and I would be allowed to visit her in the future. It was difficult for someone of my age to understand how a favourite relative could be treated like this.

I was at that school for nearly two years, and doubtless it would have been longer, but for the intervention of a repetitive ear ache. The matron told me to be brave and stop complaining. She prescribed a Bex powder, but a week later it was diagnosed as an acute mastoid. I was rushed to the Children's Hospital in Camperdown for an operation, and then caught Scarlet Fever, so it became a stay of several months.

It was in that hospital I met my first girlfriend. We were both aged seven and, as we recovered, acquaintance was made by shining mirrors at each other. Our 'romance' became an item that somehow made the pages of a Sydney newspaper, how we'd both been seriously ill, close to death, but love and flirtation by mirrors had won through. An aunt kept the clip and gave it to me years later. It must have been an afternoon tabloid, with a soap-opera story like that.

A relative visited hospital and met her. "Quite a nice girl... for a Catholic," was the comment. It was the first time I'd heard such a remark, but was to hear it frequently as this became typical of those days. Today people from other countries with different beliefs are unfairly disparaged or attacked. Back then it was our own religions that caused divisions; it even split the Labor Party, and caused tremors in sport, alienating Don Bradman and Bill O'Reilly, who both played for Australia but, it was said, would never pray together.

At least in our house religion was not a family problem. Our dad once suggested we attend Sunday School. "Fair Go, Dad," we all said in chorus, and the subject was dropped. Years later, in the army, the choice on Sundays was *attend church parade or peel potatoes in the cookhouse*. I chose the potatoes.

After the long stretch in Camperdown hospital it was decided I should resume boarding school, but my father vetoed the mountains; I think the matron's diagnosis prompted that. Instead it was Knox Grammar on the north shore. I was nearly nine when I went to the prep school there. It was an improvement, no distant dunnies; the only memory is the number of Easter holidays, when the Elf decided it was rather inconvenient for me to come home for this short break. Friends went to their distant homes in all parts of the state, while my journey was barely an hour by train, but I spent each Easter isolated in the otherwise empty boarding school. It marked me as being "different", which is not a good feeling at that age.

From the start there was always a rift between us. When I grew older I understood why I'd been sent away so early. I was the one who'd had two years of loving care from our biological mother. The twins, barely five months old when she died, could not be expected to remember her. In contrast, possibly in defiance, I treasured photos of her, idolised what I knew of her success at school, and was reluctant and uncomfortable with her replacement. It is fair to say she disliked me, because I came to resent her, and this was obviously apparent.

But in 1939, when I was twelve and the war began, there was a lot to resent. It was my first realisation the Elf was an anti-Semite. I'd long known Bah and my grandfather were Jewish, now I began to hear the perplexing murmurs of racial abuse. At the start it was a puzzle to me, the whispers, the sly hints. Soon it became difficult to talk to them without having the subject twisted to her viewpoint. Persecuted Jews were fleeing from Nazi Germany, and like asylum seekers ever since, the majority of Australia did not welcome the influx. She used this tide of opinion to disparage them. My father didn't say a lot, but nor did I ever hear him oppose her views. I felt she was trying to make him regret his first marriage. Even now I don't know why my dad listened, but he did.

Inured to family separation, I came to accept Knox. I loved sport, and in my last two years played in the cricket and rugby teams. I was a lousy student, which in hindsight I regret, but it was an uneasy time to be at school. From the age of twelve our country was at war and not winning it. Hitler's troops were rampaging all through Europe. Then Japan attacked Pearl Harbour, and their armies took only weeks to occupy half of Asia. When they were in New Guinea, much of our school conversation was no longer about football or cricket, but about what would happen, and how to escape if Japan invaded us. After they bombed Darwin, attacked the Sydney waterfront with midget submarines, and their army kept moving closer in New Guinea invasion seemed almost certain.

At fifteen I sat for the Intermediate Certificate with trepidation, which proved to be an accurate assessment of my prospects. My pass was 4 B's, the lowest possible. I was also accused of being overly fond of an attractive housemaid who worked at the school. This was reported to my father, as one of the reasons for my dismal results. It led to a lecture on the opposite gender, and how, later on, in due course and the fullness of time, I'd meet the right girl. Then feeling he'd sorted out my domestic life, we discussed the future. What did I want to do?

That was an easy answer. Fed up with ten years of boarding, I was determined to leave, and after the exam and my father hearing of supposed exploits with the housemaid, there was no parental resistance.

"Going where? To do what?" he asked.

"To Queensland, to be a jackaroo." It was a sudden impulse, a two day train journey, far enough away from Lakemba, the Elf, and life in that house. I think I was swayed by poems like *Clancy of the Overflow.*

The sheep station where I went to work was called Claverton Downs, half a million acres on the Warrego River. At first sight it looked like nirvana, but I soon learned paradise had a downside. The manager was a bullying martinet, a true Captain Bligh of the outback. It took only weeks to realise I'd never meet with his approval. To him jackaroos were city slickers to be treated with disdain. The day he told me to go into a crow trap and kill all the birds in there was the day I rebelled. I was given a wooden club with orders to stay inside the wire cage until I'd slaughtered them. I told Captain Bligh that while I knew they were nasty vicious pests, we'd each made a serious blunder. His error was to imagine I'd kill the crows, and my mistake was to imagine I'd ever be a jackaroo. I told him that since the age of twelve, despite family scorn, I'd really wanted to be a writer, a statement that produced a gaze of bog-eyed incredulity.

"A writer. What the hell's that? You mean join the fucking navy?"

I tried to explain some writers put words on paper, which was my hopeful intention.

"Yer must be totally raving mad," declared this old bush bully. "You'll never in a blue moon earn a crust doing shit work like that." He then pointed out I'd be going nowhere until the cost of my train fare was recouped. The firm that owned Claverton paid fares, on condition that jackaroos stayed twelve months. My rustic career had lasted less than four. When it had been repaid with work to his satisfaction, I got the train to Cunnamulla, hitch-hiked to Bourke, then Bathurst and back to Sydney.

My father was not thrilled to see me. The Elf barely said hello. When I told him writing was my first choice and Queensland had just been a detour, he passed judgement on my sanity. Trying to be helpful he suggested the local bank, where one of his patients was the manager. A lifetime job, he said. A lifetime of sheer hell was my feeling. He asked me to see another friend of his, a psychiatrist, who might be able to help.

To keep the peace I agreed to see the shrink. It started well. He said my lousy school results might have been caused by boarding at so young an age. After probing into the early death of my mother, and its effect, he quizzed me on feelings for the Elf, saying it was in confidence, and to please be candid. So I was extremely candid, after which he stared at me for some time.

"A difficult childhood," he eventually said. I thought he was on my side, but should have known better. His last words to me were "it's time to be sensible, and realise there's no market in Australia for you would-be writer-chappies."

I didn't care for his opinion of 'Writer Chappies'. Nor did I like his report that I was shown. He told my father I'd come to my senses and eventually take a proper job, but first I should go ahead and try to write, as I would certainly fail.

A distant relative knew someone in *The Herald*, and got me an interview with Rupert Henderson, the CEO of the Fairfax empire in those days. A career in journalism was instantly ruled out. In Mr Henderson's reign, no one was employed without a University degree. My brothers were now boarders at Knox, so apart from their school holidays, I lived alone in the dreary divide we'd occupied since childhood, trying to write short stories. If the afternoon newspapers liked them, they paid two guineas on acceptance. I tore up most of these stories rather than waste a stamp on them, sending only the one I felt the most promising to the *Daily Mirror*. It arrived back with the crushing reply: *The Editor regrets.*

My father became impatient. He said he'd make an appointment with the bank manager. I hastily declined with thanks, and obtained a job as a messenger at radio station 2GB. On hearing this my dad found it difficult to keep his temper. He said I was a lunatic. Also a disgrace. The thought of having to tell his peers, patients, or golf partners, that his son had embarked on a career as a messenger, was a serious social setback.

In 1943 Macquarie-2GB occupied a large building in Philip Street, with offices and recording studios. Radio was big time. The war had stopped the flow of imported programmes, and 2GB now made the necessary replacements, employing many actors and a small group of writers. It was why I applied for the job, prepared to run messages while trying to learn how to write radio scripts. I'd leave home early each day, catching the 6.00 train to Wynyard, then walk up the almost empty city to reach Philip Street before seven. By doing this I could borrow a typewriter, and work on stories set in romantic places like London, New York or Monte Carlo. Two hours later, when the staff arrived I'd begin my real job of running messages. These were mostly calls at pubs and tobacconists, to pick up beer and cigarettes for the senior 2GB executives. In wartime such luxuries were short, and favoured customers got special deals from under the counter. As a result, I came to know most of the sly grog merchants and black marketeers all over Sydney.

I also came to know actors and a few writers, in particular Richard Lane, who generously found time to help me. He lent me his scripts and, thank God, persuaded me to give up London, New York, or Monte Carlo, and instead write about places and people I knew. It was the start of a life-long friendship between us.

At night I'd go home and work on short stories using the clacking old Royal portable I'd bought at a pawn shop. Because of the early train departure and late arrival home, I rarely saw the Elf or my father. When I did see him, he invariably reminded me a bank would've been a lifetime job, a gullible belief in those days

"Did I think," he asked, "that I'd have a lifetime job at 2GB?"

"Good God," I said, "I hope not."

But meanwhile I was learning from Richard Lane. Nothing my dad said could prevent me writing. Even the story editor, Juan Cortez, who'd been scornful of my efforts, had begun to say one or two scripts were starting to show promise. And promise is an exciting word when you're almost seventeen. It was a lonely existence, with my brothers now much of the year at boarding school, but I might've stayed there despite the solitude, except for an ugly occurrence a few months later.

The weekly house cleaner named Freda abruptly gave notice. This was no surprise; the cleaners often left, because of the way the Elf fussed about the house, but I was puzzled soon afterwards to receive a letter she sent to me at 2GB. It contained her address, and asked if we could have a private meeting. The following day at her house in Campsie, she produced an old shopping bag full of photographs.

"It's why I quit," Freda said. "Just left her a message that I didn't like the job, and was leaving." She tipped out the contents on her kitchen table. The photographs, over twenty of them, were all pictures of my mother with her head missing. I felt sick with the shock. It was barely possible to tell if Faith, my mother's name, was alone, or with friends in these vandalised snapshots. There was one where she sat holding the twins soon after their birth; even in that her face was snipped off, to leave an empty space between their happy faces.

Freda had found the bag in our garbage bin. It had been full, and she'd tried to make room in the bin because the council rubbish truck was due, as she told me. "So I pulled the bag out to make more space, and saw the photos. It's why she put them there. After the truck took the garbage away we'd never have known about this. Sorry I had to show you. But I could hardly show your Dad, could I?"

I hid the bag, lying awake for hours that night, wishing I'd never seen the photos and wondering what to do. The only idea I could think of was trying to scare her. Let her know that I'd found out, and might tell others. I wanted to frighten the evil bitch.

Next morning I went to the nearest public phone, called 2GB to say I'd be late, then waited until my father left on his day calls and hospital visits. We had an incinerator in the back garden. I collected old rubbish and newspapers, then lit a fire and shut the lid to produce smoke. Within minutes there was a complaining voice as she came to ask what I was doing. I didn't reply to her protest it would spoil the washing on the clothes line, just produced the shopping bag, making sure it was in full view, watching her face as I took out the photos. After a moment of shock, she tried to feign innocence.

"What are those? Where did they come from?" I didn't answer, just kept feeding them into the fire, until I heard her going into the house and the back door slamming. I went to work, and that night told them I was leaving, moving to Potts Point where my grandparents lived. I'd phoned Bah, avoiding the true reason, and it was all arranged. My father was startled, and wanted to know why.

I just said I was sick of the daily train travel, and wanted a change. In the argument that followed I pointed out I'd just turned seventeen, and could choose where I lived. On this the Elf seemed to agree.

"When do you want to leave?" she asked.

"Tomorrow," I said, then added something I hoped would scare her. "I'm all packed. Even kept a couple of photos, to remind me of what happens here."

They both stared at me for different reasons. She was nervous and seemed quietly furious. He was frowning and puzzled.

"What on earth are you talking about?" he asked.

"She knows," I said, pointing at the Elf.

"Don't speak about your mother that way," he said angrily.

I'd been wanting to say it for years, so I just blurted it out. "Dad, she's not my mother. Never has been, and never will be."

The row that followed created a gulf between us that lasted for years. After some unpleasant, anti-Semitic remarks, she left, slamming the door of her bedroom. My father knew I'd upset her, but he didn't know why. Nor did I ever tell him, and I'm sure she didn't. I left the next day, and never spent a night in that house again.

Macleay Street in Potts Point was an exciting place to live in 1944, when I was seventeen. Kings Cross was a revelation after the western suburbs, a lively cosmopolitan village where many actors and artists seemed to live. It was a very different world, and a new chapter in my life began. My grandparents lived on the top floor of a three storey building with a view of Sydney harbour. It remained such a fond memory that I used it in my novel, *Against The Tide,* written as a home for the holocaust survivor, Sarah Weismann. It was extraordinary when writing about it; I could still visualise every room, even down to the furniture. As I described Sarah's life there, I felt the warmth and love I'd known fifty years earlier.

Trolley buses ran regularly to the Cross with its colourful coffee shops, kiosks, flower stalls, and lavish food stores, that

I soon learned were called delicatessens. There was a local playhouse, the Minerva Theatre, where my Gran and I went to the opening night of each new play. It was made the more exciting by having my first radio script accepted, doubtless in self-defence by the 2GB editor, as I'd regularly deluged him with scripts. After that nothing else happened for the next few months. My grandfather showed little interest in these attempts to write. I suspect he felt I'd be better off working in a bank, but he put up with my tenure of the spare room. Whereas Bah sympathised about short stories returned with regrets, and worried about rejected radio scripts. I think it was her belief that kept me stubbornly refusing to give up, until one of Sydney's afternoon papers sent a cheque for two guineas accepting a short story, then 2GB agreed to take another fifteen minute radio drama, and that was the start of it.

I was still at 2GB, but no longer running messages. Promoted to the publicity department, I was assistant and general dogsbody to a woman who wore extraordinary hats, and had scarlet nails that resembled talons. Miss Hamilton was a perfectionist and not an easy person to work for, but the move meant my wages rose from thirty shillings to three pounds a week. By then I'd had two more radio scripts produced, but told not to expect extra pay because I was already on an adequate salary. It made no difference to me. The thrill of hearing my words spoken by actors was still new. Not yet eighteen, I was even asked to write a script by another radio station. It happened because I went for a lunchtime beer with Dick Lane, to a pub that did not bother to ask the age of clients, and a producer from 2UE there. He suggested I try an episode of *Officer Crosby*, starring actor Marshall Crosby as a genial copper. They liked it, and asked me to do a few more, paying real money. The fees were modest, radio fees were notoriously stingy, and short dramas only paid three pounds per episode, but to me in those days it felt like riches.

In time this fringe activity became known at 2GB, and I was duly called to front the General Manager. It was like fronting a headmaster; he rebuked me about writing for the enemy, even though it was done at nights in my spare time, then he changed character, became cordial, and broke the astonishing news of a promotion. From now I'd be called the junior script writer, and assigned to work with Maurice Francis, who had devised the famous thriller serial *First Light Fraser*.

Maurie was something of a legend, writing a phenomenal number of serials for radio. He managed this by rapid dictation to a queue of secretaries. As one left the room with a shorthand pad full of dialogue to be typed, another would enter and he'd switch to a new serial with quite different characters. I had no part in that, but learned radio production from him, and wrote scripts for the Network. Then I had another valuable experience. Francis wrote a play for the theatre, and I was appointed the assistant stage manager, unpaid but thrilled to be involved. The stage manager with whom I became enduring friends, was Jim Russell, the gifted comic strip artist, who produced daily episodes of *The Potts* throughout his long life.

The play unfortunately was not a success. It toured small theatres and did not attract large audiences. There was a cast of seven, and one night only six people turned up to see it. We had to part the curtain and tell them the rule; if the audience numbered less than the cast, they were entitled to vote for it to be cancelled, and get their money back. Would they prefer this? The verdict was no, they wanted to see the play, so it was performed by the seven actors to an audience of six. It closed within a month, but left me with wild dreams of writing a stage play some day.

Meanwhile living in Macleay Street came to an abrupt end. In April 1945 I turned eighteen, and received my call-up. Two days later we recruits were in the training camp at Cowra. Wake-up was at a time called reveille, when a sergeant bellowed at us to "rise and shine, you lazy lot of no-hoper bastards!" Beds were made, blankets folded, and before sunrise we were in the shower block. It was not a bit like life in Macleay Street.

Drill occupied the first weeks; we learned to march in step, how to carry rifles, and told it was an offence not to salute officers. After that there were route marches and learning to shoot. Then how to fix bayonets and charge at straw figures, thrusting steel into the stomach of these scarecrows who were meant to be enemy soldiers. As weeks passed the training moved up a notch; there was barbed wire to crawl through, and machine guns firing live bullets close above our heads. This was only kid's stakes, we were told; the reality was waiting for us in New Guinea.

The army instructors were mostly veterans of World War One, who seemed to enjoy alarming us. We were shown newsreels of Kokoda, the jungle where we'd soon be facing a ferocious enemy who had lethal snipers and exploding grenades. We were also reminded to make our wills and write last letters home… just in case. I never understood what the army gained by constantly frightening the shit out of us, and it was fortunate we didn't have to face the reality. In August came the atomic bombs, with their horrific death toll, and the delay, while the world waited for the Japanese Emperor, who took another full week to agree on a surrender.

Perhaps in relief at being spared the fighting, I joined the occupation force. To my surprise there was an army broadcast section, and I was assigned to it. We sailed to Japan on a rusty old liberty ship, and while some luckier groups were situated in towns along the Inland Sea, our unit was based in the port of Kure. It was not an encouraging first sight; the harbour was a vista of twisted girders and bomb craters, but after disembarking we were agreeably surprised to be billeted in a large house well away from the waterfront. Here, amazingly, each of us had our own single room. The studio was just a short walk from there, and, within a week, the station was on air with news bulletins, music programs, relays from Radio Australia, and sports broadcasts. We were an independent small group, not many more than a dozen of us. Being so few, we had multiple roles. I was writer and announcer, doing a daily shift on air as well as writing any scripts required. We also had to assume army titles. It seemed a joke when I was named the 'transport officer.'

"But I can't drive," I said.

Our unit driver was assigned to teach me. After some kangaroo hops trying to start the jeep, I got the hang of it and began to feel full of confidence. Far too much confidence the day when I increased speed, and collided with a "honey cart." These were vehicles that emptied all the outdoor lavatories in rural Japan, and were notorious for their odour. Attempting to drive past and avoid the stink, I cannoned into the back of it at full speed. The collision emptied its malodourous cargo over the Japanese driver, as well as over our jeep, including me and my instructor. Apologies had to be made, hot showers were an urgent necessity, and I was promptly relieved of further transport duties.

Kure was not many miles from Hiroshima, and the day a few of us went there and saw what the atomic bomb had done was a sight I've never been able to forget. It was only a few months after the bomb. Hiroshima had been a large thriving city, now it was blackened and dead. Trams and traffic had been in full flow that morning; seconds later they and everyone in the streets were vaporised and ceased to exist. Over 80,000 people had been killed instantly. 70,000 more were to die from radiation sickness before the new year. At our age the impact of this destruction by one solitary bomb was devastating, a frightening realisation of what had been created. That day in Hiroshima made me anti-nuclear for the rest of my life. So too, did its poignant aftermath.

It happened on a cold wet day. We were warm inside our studio with an oil heater, when someone noticed a small boy outside trying to shelter from the rain. One of the technicians who could speak some Japanese brought him inside to the warmth, where he took off his shirt to dry. That was when we saw his back. The skin was ripped raw, as if he had been lashed by whips. We learned he'd been in Hiroshima that day. All his school friends and his entire family were dead. From that time, in constant pain, he'd survived, existing on food he found in rubbish bins. He was eight years old and had severe radiation sickness. We did our best to look after him, gave him food, took him to the base hospital, but we were told nothing could be done. Nobody knew how to treat this sickness. The doctors were surprised he'd lived so long. People in close proximity were terrified it might even be catching. Years later I wrote an article about it for the *Financial Review* in Australia, and *The Guardian* in England. I tried to express how I felt.

"For me, from that day, the tragedy of Hiroshima was not an annihilated city in which thousands died within seconds of the explosion. It was, and will forever be, the face of a damaged child, wringing wet, hungry, and dying a little more each day."

I spent 18 months with the occupation force in Japan, and came back to Australia in the winter of 1947 aged twenty. By then I'd had enough of army routine. Not that we had strict discipline; we lived like civilians, but there were rules and the occasional idiot, like a new major who took over our unit, and promptly ordered a parade for next Saturday afternoon. "But we'll be on the air," we told him.

"You'll be on parade," he told us. "The station will close down for two hours and everyone will attend."

"But Sir," the senior engineer tried to protest, "it's the weekend sports show. There'll be football on relay from Melbourne and Sydney."

"Did you hear me," the Major said. "You will shut down and be off the air from 1400 hours. You'll parade with full kit and rifles."

Rifles? He had to be joking. We'd seen no rifles since coming to Japan. We tried to tell him we didn't even know where they were.

"Find them," he ordered. "And when you have, then clean them!"

Nobody had cleaned a rifle in a year. Or drilled with one for even longer. It was a ludicrous sight. Talk about a rag-time army, out of step, and out of our comfort zone. We were hopeless. To top it the mad Major had invited the Brigadier to take the salute. Witnessing our display the Brig was furious. He went back to his quarters to listen to the Rugby.

That's when he found there was no broadcast, the Major had shut down the station. The Brig went ballistic. There were complaints from troops all over Japan about missing the sports show. The Major was promptly transferred to somewhere far off, and we were told to put our rifles back in storage. The Brigadier said he liked hearing us on radio, but never wished to see us trying to perform like soldiers again.

Japan had been interesting. It was like an incident in my life, the first sight of another country, weekends along peaceful beaches on the Inland Sea, and a riotous week spent in Tokyo. But it was time to get back to Australia, and find out whether I still had a life as a writer.

*****

PART TWO: LOVE AND A LIBRARY

Sydney, in 1947, was a place of beer shortages and blackouts. I went to 2GB in hope, but they had a full staff and no place for a junior writer. Instead I could be a part-time announcer in Wollongong, one of their network stations, but I said no thanks and moved on. It was also time to move habitat. There was a discrepancy between my grandmother's warm welcome and my grandfather's polite greeting, so I took the hint and found a cheap rental in Kellett street, Kings Cross. In those days it was a place where tarts plied for custom, and cops met crooks for financial exchanges. My room was on the top floor, a tiny bed-sitter with a sink, a gas ring, and a small table. The bathroom along the hall was shared by the tenants on our floor. By then I'd begun to realise it might not be easy to resume my career. With established writers back from war service radio was getting along without me.

I tried to exist by writing short stories, a difficult thing to do, but doubly so in Australia at that time. The afternoon tabloids in Sydney still paid only two guineas, so it was an uphill battle. My room, that the landlady called a flatette, had a slot in the door for personal mail. The thud as a heavy envelope hit the floor was certain to be a story returned with the editor's regrets, whereas the soft landing of a letter could mean the advent of a cheque. Such blessings very were rare, so I took various part-time jobs to pay the rent.

While living there I met Marjorie Crane at a blind date organised by her sister. A disastrous night all round, as I arrived after a session with army mates at the long bar in the Hotel Australia. It was the era of the notorious six o'clock closing when everyone rushed their final drinks, which is why I slept through the musical we'd come to enjoy. I woke in time to escort her home, but any chance of a goodnight kiss was out of the question, and so was the possibility of another encounter.

Years later I wrote about it in an anthology to raise funds for Pen International. We were invited to describe how we'd found a partner, or as they phrased it in their invitation: *In the sweet, funny or downright weird ways, tell us how you found love.* So I accepted the challenge, and this is a brief précis of what happened next.

A week later I was at Double Bay, about to take a tram to a party when I saw her again. She was alone, entering the cinema, where she bought a ticket for the dress circle. I forgot the party, hurriedly bought a ticket then raced upstairs. The film had started; she was in the front row and, by amazingly good fortune, there was an empty aisle seat beside her. Avoiding the usherette with her torch I managed to sit there unnoticed, for her eyes were fixed on the screen where Humphrey Bogart had just arrived in an old river boat. All through *The African Queen* her gaze never veered from the antics of Bogart and Katherine Hepburn. Not until there was a dramatic moment, with Bogie and Kate in peril from a German boat, when I got a nudge in the ribs.

"I knew it was you," she said. "Saw you waiting for a tram."

"Did you?"

"Yes. Thought you might be going to The Gap, to jump off."

"That's not very nice. I want to apologise for last week."

"Shh!" said a voice behind us. "Apologise in your own time."

"I ruined our first date," I said, ignoring this request.

"Our only date," was her answer.

"Will you two kindly shut up," hissed the voice loudly this time.

I twisted in my seat to explain matters. "Sorry, we're trying to sort out a slight problem. Actually not slight – a quite serious problem."

"Just shut up." She was a nice elderly lady with immaculate blue rinse hair, who seemed about to turn feral. Beside me my blind date got the giggles, clapping a hand over her mouth to suppress it. On an impulse I held her other hand. It was soft and warm, and wasn't snatched away. Half our attention became divided between looks at each other, and what was on the screen. When the credits began we had an identical thought; to leave before the lights embarrassed us. Down the stairs, across the road, to the tiny local beach. There was a question I wanted to ask her.

"If you saw me, why did you sit beside an empty seat?"

For a moment she just looked at me. Then the look became a smile. A lovely smile. "I thought it might be interesting," she said.

There was a full moon that seemed to hang over Middle Head as the tide lapped in. It felt so romantic it made us laugh. Her laughter was like music, her face was animated, and this seemed the moment to admit I was a first class dill, and to ask if we could start again.

A few months later we began to live together. It created a degree of frisson in her family who, despite this, invited us to Sunday lunches which became our staple meal of the week. But they were uneasy about their daughter *living in sin* as it was labelled then, and even worse, shacked up with an impoverished writer. My father merely shrugged and tried to ignore the situation. My life was turning out as his shrink had predicted: I was on a downward path to failure. And if the Elf had any say in it, probably on my way to hell.

Marjorie.

The following year we went to a small church in Bondi and were married. Her parents came to the ceremony, glad the matter was being legalised. Mine were not invited as my Dad would not have come alone, and there was no way I wanted the Elf there. Our financial situation was low but we had enough for a three-day honeymoon; a ferry ride across the harbour to a room in Manly. *Seven miles from Sydney and a thousand miles from care* was the famous slogan for this seaside suburb, with its majestic pine trees along the ocean front. I remember the pines; trustingly we left our belongings there when surfing, which was how a three-day honeymoon became two days. We went for a swim and returned to find our belongings and money had been nicked.

It was back to Kellett Street and part-time work, sorting mail or whatever was available, as radio was becoming even more of an uphill battle. Meanwhile Marge returned to her secretarial job, and some exciting news. Her boss owned a horse named Foxzami, and she'd been told it was a chance to win the Melbourne Cup. The price with off-course bookies was a generous fifty to one, so she proposed we put her week's wages on it? Fifty times her salary of seven quid – we'd be filthy rich! I talked her out of it, and the horse won. Even worse, it won easily.

That year Doris Fitton's brave venture, the Independent Theatre, opened with an Australian play, Sumner Locke Elliott's *Rusty Bugles*. It was a rare chance to see locals on stage, and for us, with friends in the cast, a chance to do it from free seats. It was a realistic play about army life, and remembering my time in training camp, the dialogue felt strong and natural. It was the night when police from the vice squad arrived to take notes about the language. I remember actors freezing for a moment on stage, then mutters from an audience stunned by this sight. The play was in danger of being banned, and only saved by Doris prevailing on Sumner to delete some of the colourful lines. We saw the play again months later, stripped of many good laughs, which actor friends told us were removed at the direction of the Chief Secretary's office. It is unfortunate that some politicians, unsympathetic to the arts, are frequently chosen to rule on these issues.

To me censorship was a scourge too often misused. Our country was adept at banning books. Among them, *Brave New World* by Aldous Huxley, *Another Country*, James Baldwin, *Borstal Boy*, Brendan Behan, were all victims. *Age of Consent*, that I adapted for the screen was a banned book not long ago. Robert Close had the humiliation of having to sit in court while his book, *Love Me Sailor*, was read to the jury by the Counsel for the prosecution. It was bad enough being forced to hear the lawyer's first monotonous reading, but there was a mistrial, so he had to suffer hearing it read again to a second jury. My wife and I were friends with Bob years after this torment occurred. His book and the treatment of it was something he could not forgive. He lived the rest of his life in Paris and Majorca.

From talk of banned books to owning a library. It was the first year of our marriage and municipal libraries were not yet established in most suburbs. I was finding it harder than ever to make a living as a writer, so we obtained a loan and bought a small lending library in Queen Street, Woollahra. This was the first of our two ventures that turned out to be self-inflicted debacles. Today Queen Street is full of stylish shops, but in 1949 it was a district of cheap rentals. Our library was miniscule, the size of a small room, where new books could be borrowed for a shilling a week, and old ones for sixpence. Not a rapid way to make a living, as eager book sellers arrived almost as often as our customers. New novels had to be bought to satisfy the clientele, but it took weeks of lending them to even recoup the cost.

I was trying to run it, but Marge arrived in her lunch hour to help when she could. We lived on the smell of an oil rag. Lunches were budgeted at sixpence. At the fish shop opposite where we bought chips, we discovered two bags at threepence each meant extra chips that way! Poverty was teaching us new tricks. We even found a cheaper place to live, at distant Avalon. This time a proper flat, even if it was just two rooms at the back of a holiday bungalow. In those days Avalon was a tiny village, containing only a corner shop and a small cinema, with a scattering of seaside houses. It was also a long and tiring trip to our library in Woollahra. Some days the earnings barely paid the bus fare, so we came to a logical conclusion. Defeated by the tedium of it, we sold the library and paid back the loan. Freed of the daily trip we went fishing, regularly catching our dinner, and only left Avalon when my brother David, now studying law and working as an articled clerk, found us a modest flat to rent in North Sydney. I even managed to get some work, ghost-writing a radio serial for a well-known writer about to take an overseas trip. The show was called *The Golden Colt*, and despite the fiasco of the Melbourne Cup, I assured him I knew all about horse racing.

We hoped he'd find Europe fascinating and stay for months, as the ghost writing would end with his return. As a bulwark we thought it best to have another sideline, and, in a partnership with George Richards, a friend from 2GB days, we became owners of a suburban newspaper. *The Mosman Chronicle*, as we called it, was a weekly tabloid, dependent on advertisements from local shops to sustain it. This, without a doubt, was our second dumb and doomed debacle.

We were crazy, of course. Our opposition, *The Mosman Daily*, was a powerful presence in the district. For years it had been flung over fences, even in pouring rain. So we decided the only way to be competitive was to put our paper in every letter box. At least they could read ours if there was a deluge.

We bought a clapped-out Ford at a bargain price because it had a faulty second gear, and other problems. Despite this we drove to our printer in Burwood each Thursday to collect the weekly edition. Then we walked the streets of Neutral Bay, Cremorne and Mosman, faithfully putting copies in every letter box. It was an exhausting process, somehow performed by just the four of us, George and his wife, Marge and me. We rarely finished before dawn on Friday, then it was back to our flat in North Sydney for bacon and eggs and a day's sleep. It was only later we heard this backbreaking delivery caused us to be listed as communists. Marge and I were at a Mosman Musical Society concert. A couple in front had loud voices and aired opinions to several rows around them.

"I hear we have a new weekly paper," the husband said.

"An invasion of Reds, darling." She was the one with a loudspeaker voice. "They put their rag in letter boxes, like all the communists do."

There was an election that year, and the local Liberal Party refused to advertise with us. George and I found ourselves facing what felt like a star chamber, being grilled on whether we were communists, or else secretly funded by them. It was during the days of McCarthyism in America, and the Mosman liberals were equally belligerent, openly sceptical how people our age could legally run a weekly newspaper. We left there angry and upset at the inquisition. So much for our long nights thinking it was worthwhile to keep the print dry. Soon after this Marge became pregnant, and I gladly gave up my share of *The Chronicle*. George kept it going, and even started another paper in Parramatta. For me it had been a diversion, but not much else.

*****

These unsuccessful attempts at alternate livelihoods remind me how doubtful I'd become about succeeding as a writer. At seventeen I'd been happy and confident as a pampered junior at 2GB. At twenty two there were downbeat days when it felt like a reckless ambition. I was trying to compete in a loftier market against far better known writers, and it made me feel insecure.

"No more disastrous enterprises," Marge made me promise, and by chance it coincided with a request from a radio producer at AWA. His name was Colin Craigen, and someone had told him I was soon to be a father. As a result Colin phoned me, saying in that case I needed work. He needed someone to do a hack job on an American soap opera they owned called *When A Girl Marries*. His company had about 500 episodes of this serial covering the war years, with lots of American dialogue and scenes of Yankee flag-waving, and people buying war bonds. All this had to be eliminated, and the massive 500 reduced to about 50 episodes taking place in peace time. It was truly hilarious, the way we ended up with giant strides in the story; young children grew up overnight, teenagers were suddenly married, hardly anything in a serial had ever moved that quickly, but the afternoon audience barely seemed to notice. It was a cut and paste task that could not really be called writing, but for a few months it paid the rent. Which was handy, as the owner of *The Golden Colt* had returned home, and already taken back the reins.

In October, on the verge of becoming parents, we were visiting friends and driving home in the same old cheap Ford, when it had a flat tyre. It was alarming, because childbirth was only days or even hours away. The folklore in the family is that I went in search of a roadside phone box to call the NRMA, and when I came back Marge had changed the tyre.

We then drove straight to the hospital, where she gave birth that night. All I remember of this is being told by the nurses to go home—no hanging about for the husband in those days, and next morning returned to meet our lovely daughter Lyn, who clutched my finger with her tiny hand, and made my day.

It was 1950, and the beginning of better years.

*****

PART THREE: RADIO DAYS

1950 was the harbinger of improving times. We swapped the dodgy old Ford for an almost new Renault. I met again with Colin Craigen at AWA to explain a series idea called *Two Stars and a Story*, short self-contained plays with two actors in each episode. He liked the idea, his company liked the idea of only two actors, and to everyone's surprise it worked a treat. It was my first solo series, and Colin generously gave me a *written by* audio credit on each episode. In radio days such accolades were rare.

I wrote one a week in the first year but could not have thought of all the storylines without help from Marge, who proved wonderfully inventive. AWA then wanted a second series, and after that something similar, this time called *Theatrette*. Same short story type plots with twist endings, but bigger casts. After that came a series called *Air Hostess*. The result of all this brought requests to work for Morris West, who ran a radio production firm in Melbourne, before achieving fame as a novelist.

Other good things happened. My brother David who'd found us a flat, now brought even better news. A client of their firm owned a house in Wahroonga, and wanted a tenant. Houses were scarce since the war; most came with an entry fee, known as "key money".

No key money, a modest rent and it was furnished, my brother assured us. We hurried to inspect it and found it perfect, a comfortable house, large garden and an extra miracle, a telephone. This was a real bonus: phones post-war were as scarce as hen's teeth. A friend claimed he'd won his divorce, being awarded custody of the family phone.

We moved in a week later. Lyn was at the crawling and part walking stage, one day reaching an adjacent street before we realised she was missing. Panic was avoided when a neighbour brought her home.

"I think she belongs to you," said Sidney Nolan. He lived around the corner, and we'd often exchanged waves when he was digging his vegetable garden. He and Marge had a chat about painting, while I tried to explain to our daughter the dangers of ventures abroad. The next time our roving Lyn went missing was in David Jones, Elizabeth Street branch, where we found her with a bunch of policemen who'd bought her an ice cream. She stopped roaming, aged four, and found a boyfriend next door. After that they climbed trees in our garden, and to our relief no-one fell off.

By the early nineteen fifties I was writing for other outlets, in particular Grace Gibson, an American who owned the largest radio production unit in Australia. She commissioned an idea of mine called *Medical File*, and after this *Famous Trials*, followed by *For The Defence*, both these series featuring celebrated lawyers in legendary courtroom battles. Apart from being contracted by EMI to adapt Neville Shute's book *The Far Country*, I was now hardly writing for anyone except Grace. I also wrote a thriller called *The Golden Cobweb* for her company. That was when I learned something new about her.

She said to me one day, "It's going well. What happens next?"

I said I didn't know, had no idea until I sat down at the typewriter.

She was shocked. "You really don't know? That makes me very nervous," she said. "All my writers tell me what'll happen. I like to know where we're heading, and why."

I explained that I disliked outlines, and thought plotting in advance was a destructive way to ruin a good story. I always felt that, and still do. Eventually, if reluctantly, she put up with my methods; in time even nominating *Golden Cobweb* as one of her favourites.

A lot of our radio shows now took place in overseas countries. We'd all seen so much of Britain, Europe and the USA on newsreels during the war, that foreign locations had become familiar. Writers started to feel they knew London, Berlin and Paris as well, or sometimes better, than our own cities. It was one of the reasons why Australian radio shows became popular overseas, and Grace, with her American contacts, knew foreign drama cost no more to produce. Any country was easily created on air by actors with the right accents, and if necessary a few sound effects around a microphone in her Bligh Street studio. They were a profitable sell on the world market, and few of us writing scripts realised it.

In 1953 she startled both me and the industry by asking if I would become Head of Production for her company. Though flattered, I was unsure whether to accept; it was a surprising offer, extremely well paid, more than twice what I made as a writer. But it meant strict office hours supervising dozens of shows, and having to deal with directors over twice my age. The main director Lawrence H Cecil was a veteran in his sixties, another, John Saul, was in his fifties. Luckily they were amenable when I accepted the appointment, unlike a few who did not welcome the news.

I enjoyed the job, but eventually misgivings about oppressive office hours proved correct. I worked best in early mornings and late at night, but had to be available in the office from nine to five to perform the job. Turning up late did not win many plaudits, despite working on a script for the Gibson company the previous night. So after six months I resigned. Grace tried to dissuade me, and failing this, became furious. We had a huge row until interrupted when the tea lady arrived, dropped her tray, and had a heart attack. Hostilities ceased while we sent for an ambulance, and fortunately she recovered. Our quarrel was industry news, with predictions I'd never work for Grace again. Nor would I be welcome, rumour said, at an industry party she was giving that weekend.

But her umbrage didn't last; she rang the next day and we made peace over the phone. She insisted I come to the party, and I arrived at her penthouse to the astonishment of adversaries. *"They thought I'd shot my bolt, and their faces were wonderful to behold,"* was my comment quoted by her authors James Aitchison and Reggie James. We stayed friends for the rest of her life.

Grace was a fabulous woman. She should be remembered as Australia's major producer of radio drama over three decades. Sadly she and her many achievements seem to have been forgotten.

On a joyful February day in 1954 our son Perry was born, and we felt comfortably anchored for the rest of our lives in peaceful Wahroonga. Our neighbours were all friends, the man next door had a tennis court but rarely used it, so we were invited to play whenever we wished. That was the year when the owner of our rented house decided to sell it, and gave us first offer. The price was four thousand pounds which today sounds incredible, and even then was modest. A future road was planned, and the Road Authority told us a small corner of our land might be affected. A very small corner. Hence the low price, and we gladly became owners.

Years later, long after we'd sold it, we went back to take a look with our daughter Lyn, who wanted to see where she'd spent her first five years. It was not to be. Our entire house, next door's tennis court, and half the street was now buried beneath a freeway to the Central Coast. So much for very small corners!

1954 was the year when my output became too large. If the weekends were sacrosanct for tennis or the beach, each Monday started at five a.m. I'd committed myself to writing a new thriller serial, and began early on the first episode before the family was awake for breakfast. Four episodes were needed each week, and with this early start I could write all four by that evening. Looking back it's hard to recall how I could work at this pace. The serial episodes were mostly fifteen minutes, but allowing for commercials this reduced to twelve and a half minutes. Even so, it was the equivalent of fifty minutes dialogue in a single day!

The remainder of the week was spent on two self-contained half hour scripts. One of them *Address Unknown*, was the most popular local drama at the time, the other was *For The Defence*, a courtroom drama that required research. Like most writers at that time it was a heavy workload, far too much, but the rates of pay had never kept up with the cost of living. The half hours had to compete with drama programs from England or America, yet payment was modest in comparison. Apart from higher fees, foreign writers received royalties on all their overseas sales.

Our problem was the lack of a Writers' Guild. At one stage we were attached to Actors Equity, but they could do little for the actors, let alone for us. A Guild might've prevented mistakes. Our big blunder was to be paid in cash and sign a receipt for it, not realising that by doing this we were selling world rights. None of us knew our work would become popular overseas, let alone shown there without compensation. Television writers soon learned to fight for this foreign royalty; radio never tried.

During this time of massive production, it became a contest to deliver the most scripts, and before long the inevitable happened; quantity instead of quality became the yardstick of success. The amount we were writing began to concern many of us. Each week had the same relentless pattern, and I started to feel in a rut. We had two young children, and I was too busy, or too tired to spend enough time with them.

Trying to rectify this, I resigned from the serial and sought an increased fee for *Address Unknown*. I got half of the rise I'd asked for, on condition I didn't spread the news. The only news that spread was my decision to quit halfway through a popular serial, and offer it to someone else. This caused bewilderment among other scribes. Nobody gave up work by choice. "Are you ill?" one friend wanted to know.

Not ill, I told him. Just sick of writing too much, and feeling on a treadmill. Plus wanting to spend more time with my kids. There was no way they were going to have a deprived childhood like mine.

The following year, 1955, there was an elephant in the room. Television was imminent. The Menzies government did the obvious, awarding the commercial licences to media moguls Packer and Fairfax. Frank Packer (Kerry's father) declared his intentions. At a public hearing in March 1956, he announced there were no actors or writers in the country ready to work in television. Questioned on this by Clive Evatt for Actors Equity, Packer said "I'll treat Australians how I've always treated them."

Let me out of here, I thought. But there was more. He said audiences would not be keen to view local shows, so it would be essential to import programs. The inference was that home content could cover the news and weather forecasts. It was alarming to think that when television drama usurped radio, which in time it most surely would, we'd all be headed for the scrapheap.

I went home and said to Marge, "Let's go to England".

"Right," she said, without the blink of an eyelid. "When?"

It was her calm certainty that made it seem possible, but that same night we realised two obstacles lay ahead. The first was our young children, ages five and two. The second was finance. We worked out what we had in the bank, discovering the balance was less than we thought. But that was not the main cause for concern. Income Tax was the major hurdle, a very large problem indeed. In those days you couldn't leave the country without a tax clearance.

We had to go soon, before the kids became settled into school, or it would be too late. That meant we had to go this year. Day and night it became all we could think about. We felt it had to happen. The problem was how?

For a start we committed ourselves by paying a small deposit for a four berth cabin on an Italian ship, the *Fairsea*. Her next voyage when she returned from the UK was in August, only three months away, so we had to do everything very fast. We rented our Wahroonga house, and moved to a cheap out of season cottage in Collaroy. I worked all hours taking everything offered, devised a new thriller serial called *Rick O'Shea* and wrote the first dozen episodes. The rest would be written on the ship and overseas, providing a modest lifeline for the first months. The 1956 Olympics was to take place in Melbourne, and a special radio series called *Olympic Flame* was launched to mark the occasion. I was asked to write the pilot episode by producer Hans Adlerstein, a close friend for whom I'd written many previous scripts. Hans aided our cause with a very substantial payment.

Meanwhile Marge was adapting American scripts for Grace Gibson. Grace had tried to talk us out of going, at first, then decided we were serious, so she helped with this friendly gesture. Everything had become possible when my brother David offered to go guarantor for our tax clearance. It was a favour we never forgot. That was the day we sold the car and paid the balance for our cabin. By now people were airing the opinion that we were mad. They didn't know quite how mad; apart from David, no-one else knew we only had one-way tickets, and no return fare.

Even unaware of this, there was major concern from relatives and some friends. The children were surely too young. Others asked, what if there was no work? How would we live? Surely it was a risk? Yes, we were aware of the risk, but too young to care, too excited to listen or think for a moment it might be a massive mistake. My one concern was my grandmother who had not been well recently. We spent a day with Bah to say goodbye, when she assured us it was only a minor illness. She put us at ease, making us promise to keep in touch with frequent letters.

On the last day I rang my dad using his surgery phone, so the Elf would not take the call. He'd heard the news, and was not impressed.

"Taking young children that age overseas. You must be around the bend" he said, "if you know what that means."

"It means I'm nuts," I said. "You've been reading Nevil Shute, who made that expression popular."

"I heard it on the radio," he replied. "Better than most rubbish."

"Nice of you to say so, Dad. I adapted it."

"That's why I listened," he replied, then repeated I was a fool to go overseas when I had plenty of work here. He hung up before I could reply, leaving me sorry I'd waited until the last day to make this call. With more time we might have met, and had a chance to mend relations. Although the Elf factor might've prevented that.

On the following cold August day we boarded the *Fairsea* at Woolloomooloo. It was a one class ship with lots of people about our age, some to study, others to take jobs or tour. Britain had no work visas then, so none of us needed permits. David came to bid farewell, and Ray Barrett arrived with a bunch of actor friends. Ray promised he'd join us in the Old Dart, as he did a year later.

We had a four berth cabin on B deck, cramped but cosy. It was a lucky choice of ship, for Italians love children. A stewardess agreed to sit with the kids at night, and each day the captain sent his first officer to ask if Perry could join him on the bridge, where a tiny wheel awaited him. Our son stayed there to help steer the ship, and this invitation was made to him right throughout the voyage.

The Indian Ocean was tranquil, the weather sublime. Marge and I took part in the celebration when we crossed the equator. We were just two days from Suez and barely a week from arriving in England, when the Egyptian government took the shock decision to blockade the canal. It meant a long detour to South Africa, then up the west African coast, adding several weeks to the journey. Word spread we'd run out of food and grog. The food lasted; the grog was touch and go.

Amazingly my other brother Dick had been working in South Africa, and was due to be married in Durban on the same day that our Captain estimated we'd arrive there. For twenty four hours we enjoyed the thought of being surprise guests at his wedding, then reality intruded. News came that Durban harbour was full; we were diverted to Cape Town instead. We sailed past, mising their wedding by a day, and it was ten years before I saw him again, and met Mireille, his charming French wife.

Cape Town was an uneasy place. Apartheid was only six years old, but already rigidly enforced. Locals kept asking whether we had a gun; if not, don't walk in certain areas. Except for a brief visit to Table Mountain and some of the beautiful beaches, we were glad to leave there. Our next port was Tenerife in the Canary Islands, where the unspoiled Spanish ambience was a pleasant contrast. Lyn had her sixth birthday while we were in port. From there we sailed past Portugal and Biscay. Soon we were just a day from Southampton, starting to wonder what our new existence would be like.

*****

PART FOUR: ENGLAND

There is no tactful way to put it: arriving in London was one of the worst days of my life. It was such a contrast after the Italians who loved children, coming to a city where, at first, it seemed kids were unwelcome. In addition a blunder by our bank did not assist that devastating day.

After the extended voyage and close contact with so many people who'd become friends, we were suddenly on our own. Realisation of this came abruptly when we left the train at Waterloo. There, phone numbers or addresses were being exchanged, but we were unable to take part and provide one. All we had was a short-term booking in a South Kensington boarding house, organised by our Sydney bank. Half an hour later we didn't have that. We arrived to be told there was no reservation.

"The bank of New South Wales booked us rooms," I said. "We cabled them from Cape Town to advise you about the Suez delay."

"We had no word from Cape Town, or any previous booking from your bank in Sydney."

"They told us they'd received confirmation."

"Whatever they said, we have no record," was the increasingly rigid reply. "Do you realise this is Motor Show week? We're full. The whole of London is full. You've come at a very bad time."

I can still recall every single word of that chilling response. The woman who ran the place must have felt sorry for us and, in the end, did her best to help. She made a phone call and said a friend of hers could accommodate us for a brief stay, until we sorted things out. It was another guest house just two streets away, but we had to take a taxi because of heavy luggage and tired children. The cabbie was not too thrilled about such a short journey. The room on the third floor contained a double bed and two makeshift stretchers. There was no lift, so we made several trips to carry up the suitcases, while the kids sat on the top step, almost certainly wondering what other catastrophe lay ahead.

"There is just one thing," said the well-upholstered lady who ran the place, "most of my lodgers are regulars here. Single people. We can serve you breakfast, but would you mind having it in your upstairs room so the children don't disturb my guests." In my first few hours in London I came to the conclusion I would never like this city.

That evening we went to an Italian restaurant on the corner of Gloucester Road. It still exists—I've had many meals there in the years since. But that first night remains deep in my memory because it was so uncomfortable and difficult for the children. We were stressed after our reception, and they sensed it. At age two, Perry had never eaten in a proper restaurant. Nor, I realised, had Lyn. It felt a long, long way from home, and I sat there wondering what the hell I'd done to their lives. But it was too late for regrets. We were on the other side of the world, and even if we wanted, there was no possible way to go back.

We found a public phone the next day and rang Dennis Burrell, an English friend from the ship. He lived with his family in New Malden, and said he'd do his best to help. We kept our fingers crossed, because the third floor attic with breakfast on a tray was a distinctly short term proposition. We hated having to keep telling the kids to be quiet. There was nowhere for them to play; whatever the weather, we had to take them across to Kensington Gardens each day, so they wouldn't upset the regulars. They were confused and unhappy, and we knew it.

At least we thought, things can't get worse, but they did. We went to meet actor friend Bud Tingwell at his bank in Mayfair. Bud had arrived a few weeks earlier and was a client there, so we sat waiting while he met the manager. Near us was a model of a Qantas plane, perched on a table beside a large glass window. Perry was clearly entranced by the model plane, and started to play with it.

"Darling, don't do that," his mother said, but she was seconds too late. As the wing of the plane contacted the window, the glass began to crack. Marge tried to hold it intact but the huge window crumbled. *Sixty years later I can still see it in slow motion replay, this huge plate glass window dissolving into fragments and crashing alongside us.*

I wished the floor would open so we could all descend into the vault and stay there. Even worse, the bank people were very kind and understanding, anxious to console our small son that it was an accident, and assuring us it was covered by insurance. But for the next year the window remained covered by sheets of boarding, and we felt guilty each time we went past.

Thankfully Dennis came good. Friends of his family would give us accommodation for a few weeks, so we went off to New Malden. They were a kind and cheerful couple, and the house had a garden where the kids could play. There was also television which none of us had seen until then, as we left just before TV began in Australia. It was a great help keeping the children occupied; they were wide-eyed. On the first Sunday our host appeared wearing a smart jacket, with collar and tie. His wife changed to a new dress. Then the TV set was wheeled through the house to their rarely used front room. We were puzzled, until told the BBC Sunday night play would start at eight o'clock. At five minutes to eight the children were in bed, and we were in our chairs as the screen showed the title of the play and listed the cast. Music accompanied this, and on the hour the play began. I sometimes wished this formality had lasted, but perhaps without the collar and tie, for it gave television plays esteem, and was better than rushed credits that now flash past on screens.

After two weeks we found a flat in Hammersmith. The rent was slightly more than we could afford, but the prospect of living in London, the four of us in our own place at last, was irresistible. Things improved slightly. Before we left Australia my accountant said that if I had no contacts in England, why not look up Harry Alan Towers.

Towers of London, as he called his radio company, had produced the British series *Hornblower* and *Black Museum*, each starring Orson Welles. I'd met Harry who was often in Australia to sell his shows, but I doubted he'd be of use as rumour said he was now bankrupt.

"It's true," was the reply. "But by the time you get there, if I know Harry, he'll be back in business."

While it was wonderful to move to the Hammersmith flat, the rent was a strain on our finances. I was writing and posting back episodes of the O'Shea serial to Australia, eventually receiving a cheque weeks later. It was barely enough for us to live on, so one day, resolving he could only say no, I decided to ring Towers. Sure enough my accountant was right. He was not only back in business, but producing a radio series of *The Third Man*, with Orson Welles as Harry Lime.

"My dear boy," he had an odd piping voice, "do come and see me. You're in luck." We met and he contracted me to write a script. It was the last episode of the series. A thin slice of fortune in the nick of time.

In the northern spring of 1957, my grandmother died. She had been ill before we left, but assured us it was nothing serious, and convinced me she'd spend the summer in their Collaroy cottage. In our first English winter I'd often thought of her now recuperating in the hillside house where we'd shared holidays; it was not until after her death that I learned it had been cancer. I had such memories of her warmth and kindness, our mutual enjoyment of plays or films, and most of all, the years of belief and support that had assisted me. Apart from my wife and children, she was the person I loved most in my life.

I remembered promises made to her, that I'd break into television. So far I'd been coping with survival, and done little except the script for Towers, and trying to meet producers without success. It was a matter of 'show me what you've done, and if you haven't written anything then don't waste my time.' It felt like my difficult attempt to start again after the army, but this was a much tougher market, hindered by not knowing how to write for the screen, and having no contacts in the industry. The first few months had made it clear the only way to work for the BBC or the commercial ITV stations was to spend my time writing speculative plays. This meant using any money we'd saved, and staking it on the future. It was a time to be far braver than I'd been until now.

Living cheaply was a first essential. A magazine advertised a house in a Spanish village for a pound a week, and since Spain at the time had the lowest cost of living in Europe, the next problem was finding a way to get there. That was solved when we found a Wolseley car going for only sixty pounds, because it was ten years old and hell on petrol, which to our surprise, was still rationed in Britain. It was also spacious enough for the kids to sleep in, so we gave up Hammersmith, drove to Dover and took the cross channel ferry.

When the weather was good we camped most nights to save money, because the Wolseley was a true gas guzzler, and filling it with petrol in France was a big ticket item. We had a crappy little tent, a slum compared to the large canvas havens that seemed *de rigueur* for French families, but we huddled in our shanty while the kids slept in the car. It was late April and skiing was over, so the lodges were a cheap rental if it rained.

In France we drove down the Rhone Valley practising our French, then across the Pyrenees, through the border and along the Spanish coast. In response to questions from the back seat that began when we left the cross-channel ferry, asking if we were nearly there, we could now almost truthfully reply we were on the last lap. The back seat interpreted this as around the next bend, but were silenced when the Mediterranean came into distant view.

"Will we be near the sea," came Lyn's hopeful voice.

"We'll soon find out," her mother replied.

"When?" asked Perry, as if suspicious of promises.

"In about fifteen minutes," was an answer that made them both excited, trying to get the best view out the window. Marge and I shared their eagerness, anxious to know what kind of dump this cheap rent was going to look like.

The house for a pound a week turned out to be modest villa on a crescent beach. It was in a village north of Barcelona called *Sant Antoni de Calonge*. The sand was just metres from the front door, and a wide view of this pristine beach led all the way to the neighbouring town of Palamos. *Sant Antoni* was tiny in those days; a few houses on the hillside, and a sole grocery shop in the only street.

It was the first week of May and summer beckoned. The sun shone, the sea was a tranquil blue, and the beach seemed to stretch forever. The place was an unexpected paradise.

*****

We stayed almost five months. We could have stayed longer, but Lyn would be seven in October, and thoughts of school had begun to dominate. Also, we had not come across the world to be beachcombers, no matter how congenial the life. By now I'd written two speculative plays (unsold), as well as a couple of outlines for a TV series (no takers), and finished the last *Rick O'Shea* serial scripts. Payment for these and rent from the Wahroonga house had kept us solvent, for living was cheap and the locals friendly and helpful. But despite bargain rates for wine and food, money was running short. It was clear I must get an agent, for there was no real chance of selling scripts without one. Putting a private return address on offerings I'd sent to the BBC, felt like an admission of defeat. So in September 1957 we packed up, said a reluctant goodbye to Spanish friends, and set out to drive to Calais.

The plan was carefully worked out. An early start. Two days drive to Lyon, another two to the coast, and on the fourth day, if all went well, we'd be on the cross-channel ferry. But all did not go well. Our reliable Wolseley broke down on the way. We had to be towed into the nearest town, our budget punctured by the cost of repair and an extra night in a French hotel. The situation became worse when we arrived in Calais too late to catch that day's last car ferry. It meant yet another night's stay. We had just enough travel money to pay for the crossing, and get us a hotel room when we reached London. Missing the ferry was a calamity; we'd have to sleep in the car that night, and there was the problem of dinner.

We went to a restaurant near the Quai, where a study of the menu alarmed us. We had about fifteen local francs to spare, and from the prices it would not buy an *hors d'oeuvre* to share between us. A middle-aged woman approached with her pad and pencil poised to take our order.

"Madame," Marge said in her best French, "we have a problem. You see the car outside?"

The Madame looked puzzled, but agreed she could see our dusty old vehicle parked outside. She asked why was she being told this.

"We've come from Spain," Marge persevered, "and the car has used most of our money with repairs and petrol. The petrol is costly in France. So instead of us eating today, the car has been fed with fuel." She later admitted not all her French had been completely exact, but Madam's vanishing smile revealed she'd grasped the situation.

"You cannot pay to eat?" she said in English, without enthusiasm.

"We have fifteen francs," my wife said, and the French woman clicked her tongue with disappointment. "But the children are hungry, so if you can feed them, my husband and I will watch them eat."

In reply the Madame let forth a stream of words, too quick for us to understand. She pointed at the table, at the kids, at us, then marched off to the kitchen.

"What's happening?" I asked.

"Search me, I lost it," Marge said. "May as well wait and find out."

So we waited. Then her husband emerged from the kitchen. He went to the window, looked at the car, shook his head at the sight of it. "A thirsty beast," he said to us in English, and went back to the kitchen.

Soon afterwards Madame reappeared. She carried a large tureen. Her husband followed with French bread. They set the tureen full of soup on the table, then produced four bowls and four spoons. By this time we were the object of attention from the other diners.

"Eat," said Madame.

We ate as ordered. I have to say, it was the most wonderful soup I'd ever tasted. We ate plateful after plateful, soaked the baguettes in it, drained the tureen. When the Madame returned, retrieved the empty dish and showed it to her customers, the whole restaurant broke into applause.

"Was it bon?" she asked us.

"Tres bon," Marge said, overcome. Merveilleux !" She ran out of French superlatives and gave Madame a dazzling smile instead.

"Wait," we were told. She went to a wall cupboard and produced a key to unlock it. She took out four apples, placing one in front of each of us. It felt like a special Gallic moment, a memorable concord. That night we slept soundly in the car, nurtured by the food and her kindness.

We caught the ferry next morning and reached London by early afternoon. There was a modestly priced hotel in Bayswater, but literally as we reached it the Wolseley broke down again. We carried our luggage inside, then called a garage who went into detail about gaskets and damage that sounded terminal. They offered us twenty pounds for the spare parts if we wished to get rid of it. Otherwise it would be stuck in the street to collect parking fines. So we settled for twenty quid, and stood watching it towed away. It had taken us to Spain and back again; it had been a refuge in wet weather, and saved the ultimate breakdown until the last stretch of our odyssey. Never mind that it consumed petrol like an alcoholic in a wine bar, it had got us back, and we were grateful.

For perhaps the first time, we began to think of London as home.

The approach of another winter in London almost changed our minds. It was a contrast from our lovely beach in Spain, and probably the toughest winter of my life. Money was perilously short. The house rental and fees for the final radio scripts was our sole income, but the exchange rate to sterling was not in our favour at the bank. Towers had finished with radio. He was moving into film and had a stable of experienced writers; I was clearly not on the list. We tried to be cheerful keeping our fears from the children, and found a low rental flat, where I started to write yet another television play. It had to be speculative, for no-one was going to make offers to an unknown. The only place to work with a portable was on the kitchen table, so between meals I typed there while the kids made a cubby house beneath it. I'd sometimes hear my daughter say: *Shhh! Dad's working*! Our children were wonderful, the way they put up with this nomadic living.

There were some Australian writers in London at that time, but Rex Rienits was the only one who contacted us. He'd had a long career in radio, and knew the problem of switching to write for the screen. What Rex taught me I treasured and never forgot. He went on to write historical books with his wife Thea, and remained a close friend all his life. It was first Rex, then another day soon afterwards that combined to make such a difference.

I first met Spike Milligan on the fifth floor of a building above a fruit shop in Shepherd's Bush. A friend told me he had an office there.

"Strange place for an office," I said. In my ignorance of London at the time, Shepherd's Bush sounded like somewhere in the countryside.

I learned it was merely ten minutes away, where he and a group of comedy writers had formed a co-operative. "Come and meet him," the friend offered. "He likes Aussies. His parents now live in Woy Woy. He said it's so perfect they decided to name it twice."

So I went to meet Spike at Shepherd's Bush, and it looms large in my memory, for this was a day that changed my life. I met not only Spike, but a bunch of comedy writers who made me welcome and became friends. Eric Sykes was both actor and writer of his own comic sketches, Johnny Speight wrote *Till Death Us Do Part*, Ray Galton and Alan Simpson were renowned for *Hancock's Half Hour*, then wrote the marvellous *Steptoe and Son*. There was Terry Nation, who invented the Daleks, and Dave Freeman, a comedy writer for Benny Hill. Last, but certainly not least, there was Beryl Vertue, a bright young woman in her twenties, who had joined to look after the office and was now their agent.

When we met she asked if I wrote comedy.

"Drama," I said, whereupon she wondered if I had an agent.

"Not yet," I told her. She became my agent that day.

I was the lone drama writer among her stable of comedy writers, and she was, without a doubt, the best agent I ever had. She represented me for the next fifteen years, until she became a successful film and television producer. Today the same Beryl Vertue, still a close friend, is head of a production company that produces *Sherlock* and a long list of major shows.

At that first meeting she did warn me that progress could take a while, and in line with her prediction nothing happened for the next few months. In fact we began to realise were facing a bleak Christmas. Our only source of income now was what Marge earned, for Spike had asked her to type his scripts. But she and I were worried enough to secretly discuss a fall-back option; we should try to raise money for her and the kids to go home if that became really necessary, and if it did happen, then I'd follow as soon as I could. So I made an appointment with the Bank of New South Wales to request a loan.

"Impossible," said the manager. "You have no collateral. Sorry," he said, without managing to sound it.

I left Berkeley Square, walking past Bud Tingwall's bank, where the window was still covered by plywood. No hope in there, I decided, then rembered the AMP. After we married I'd been talked into an insurance policy, and until now had paid about a hundred pounds into it each year. That was at least eight years ago . . so *stuff the bank.*

"Yes, you have a policy with us," one of their minions said when I kept an urgent appointment, "but you can't borrow money on it."

"I can't? Why not?"

"It's not that sort of a policy."

"Well, what sort of a policy is it?"

"One that matures in thirty years. When you're sixty. By then..." he consulted a file, "it'll be a nice nest egg."

"By then I might be dead," I replied.

"Your widow would receive the full amount," he said cheerfully.

"Meanwhile I pay until I'm sixty?"

"That's it," he agreed.

"Well, I've got news for you. I can't pay. So what happens if I stop? There must be small print that says it can be cashed in."

"Most unwise. But it is possible," he finally admitted.

"Great. Because I've got at least eight hundred pounds."

"Good heavens, no. That's not how it works." He cheerfully went into the insurance *modus operandi* for my benefit. I learned how the early contributions paid commission to the agent who sold it to me. How real accumulation begins much later. Should I be imprudent enough to cash it, I'd receive only two hundred pounds.

"What about the rest?"

"Hold it for the full term and it will grow."

"Bugger that," I said, "I'll take the two hundred."

"You'll lose a lot."

"I'll gain a lesson— never to insure again."

Since then I've spread the word life insurance is legalised robbery, unless you die young.

Christmas came and went. The AMP's cheque provided a small amount of cheer. Beryl kept circulating my plays; rejections took about two months, and all these were rejected. At that time there was a large market for television plays; three were shown each week on the ITV network and three on the BBC. None of them were mine.

"Don't give up," Beryl said.

I sent her another play and an idea for a TV series. This caught the attention of Hannah Weinstein, an American who headed Sapphire Films. Hannah paid a small option on my series idea, based on the radio show *Address Unknown*. She was a pleasant and scrupulously fair woman, and when she couldn't raise interest in *Without a Trace,* as I'd called it, she suggested I write an episode of her BBC series *Robin Hood,* starring Richard Greene. Hannah was sympathetic to the Hollywood writers blacklisted by McCarthy. She hired many of them to write under assumed names on *Robin Hood,* so I found myself amid an illustrious group including Oscar winner Dalton Trumbo. She also paid the highest fees in British TV at the time. One thousand pounds, Beryl announced, and I could hardly believe it. After months of drought and disappointment, it was like winning lotto.

So things began to happen; some of it good like Hannah, some of it rather strange.

Beryl introduced me to a new producer, someone unknown to her, who'd contacted her by phone. He'd read one of my scripts and was enthusiastic. We had several meetings with him in Beryl's office. By then the agency had moved from Shepherds Bush to an up-market address in Kensington High Street. My agent had now graduated to a large office with a view of the main street and Kensington Gardens.

Henry Ramsden, the man so keen on my work was clearly rich, for he travelled to our meetings in a chauffeur-driven Bentley. He loved his car, spoke about it, even had a photo of it in his wallet. His chauffeur, he explained, always parked it in the side street around the corner from the agency, away from traffic and parking restrictions.

At our meetings we talked ideas, and he also talked fees with Beryl. She seemed impressed with the numbers he was quoting, while I was getting stimulated at the thought of originating a series of my own. Beryl said I was ready and eager to start work, and at this meeting he agreed he was also ready, a contract would be in the mail and I should start writing. We shook hands on the deal, and he left for a meeting with Lew Grade, the head of ATV. My proposed new show would be on their agenda. He went out to his car, after asking if he could use Beryl's phone, and telling his chauffeur he was ready to be collected.

I stayed to chat with Beryl. It felt like the moment I'd been waiting for, the real start of my career. I'd scored the interest of a rich man. He had a Bentley, a chauffeur, and a meeting with the famous Lew Grade. I could begin writing. That was the moment when Beryl's secretary rushed into her office and said to look out the window. What we saw was our would-be producer across the street, lined up at the bus stop. Where was the Bentley? Where was the chauffeur? We watched the man who was going to make me rich and famous get on a number 9 bus.

We tried to give him the benefit of the doubt. Perhaps the Bentley had broken down, but there was hardly time for that. Beryl promptly rang the phone number on his business card, which was non-existent. She was angry and upset, we were all baffled why anyone would carry on like a rich producer with a Bentley when it was fantasy. Beryl hoped for a chance to tell him what she thought of him, but he must have glimpsed us at the window, because he never turned up again.

I did see him once, almost a year later. I was in Oxford Street, buying a present in Selfridges, and he was behind the tie counter serving a customer. I didn't bother confronting him. What was the point?

But it was a setback, because he'd been so convincing and aroused high expectations. I felt depressed and began to think the script for Towers and the *Robin Hood* might be the extent of my career in England because nothing else happened for a time. Well, things did happen, but not in my stalled career.

A friendly estate agent called, offering us a better flat in Earls Court Road. Four bedrooms, a ground floor and a basement, which meant it included a garden big enough for a dog. Lyn had been pining for one ever since we had to leave a pet behind in Australia. A fourth bedroom meant no more scripts on the kitchen table. My own study at last.

Wonderful, we said, but when the end of the month came the agent was embarrassed. The owner, Mrs Worthington, had decided not to have tenants with children. I could not believe this spectre had surfaced again. It was a huge disappointment for them both; they'd been eagerly looking forward to the garden.

I felt furious. Lyn was nearly eight and doing well at school, Perry was soon to be five and at a kindergarten in Sloane Square. I told them to wash and brush their hair, then we drove to Earls Court Road and rang the bell. Mr Worthington, her son, answered the door. He was in his thirties, a plump figure in striped shirt and braces.

Before he could speak I asked him if *these two* were the reason we were unsuitable as tenants? He was so embarrassed I thought he might slam the door, but he suggested we speak to his mother. So we went upstairs, and his mother turned out to be a handsome Englishwoman in her sixties, who professed to be shocked at what the agent had said.

"I have absolutely nothing against children," she asserted.

"Dad was going to buy us a dog," my daughter said, a line I swear I didn't give her, but could've hugged her for saying it.

"Now we can't have one," Perry chimed in, and I felt they must've concocted the scenario together.

Mrs Worthington seemed captivated by these small disappointed faces. She insisted her son bring lemonade and biscuits.

"And there's a tennis court in the square across the road," Lyn told her, while drinking the lemonade. "Dad was going to teach us tennis."

In the end I didn't have to say much. It became a three way conversation between Mrs Worthington and our son and daughter. They told her how they'd been living in Spain, and how dad was a writer, and we were Australian. Mrs W said she liked Australians, and did they know the district was called Kangaroo Valley? Mr Worthington and I were an audience by this time, so he brought me a beer. We sipped while his mother asked the kids if they liked Spain. Was it strict for visitors?

"We had to go to the police station every month," they told her, "and he made us stand in a line while he inspected the passports."

"Were you scared of him?" she asked.

"At first," Lyn said. "But there was a picture of Franco on the wall behind him. While he looked at our passports, we stared at this picture, and my brother suddenly started singing *God Save the Queen*."

Mrs Worthington was open-mouthed, and close to laughter. She asked what had happened. Was he angry? Were they in trouble?

No, Lyn told her. "The policeman smiled and clapped, and we started laughing. Even the policeman laughed."

"These children are gorgeous," Mrs Worthington said to me. "I'm not the least surprised they charmed Franco's Guardia. If you don't mind, I'd love to tell my bridge club the story about God Save the Queen."

We left with promises she'd have a serious word to the estate agent who had plainly misinterpreted her wishes.

"Would you object if we had a dog?" I asked, feeling the kids had put us in a winning position.

"I love dogs," she said.

That afternoon the agent rang to say he'd misinterpreted his client's instructions. I doubted it; I think our children had won the old girl over.

We moved in the following week, and it was one of our longer and happier tenancies. It was in that flat a month later, that the phone rang one morning with miraculous news. Beryl told me a television play had been accepted by the BBC. I was so used to failure, it was hard to believe for a moment.

"Truly?" I asked.

"Truly," she insisted. "I'm absolutely thrilled. Isn't it splendid?

More than splendid, I said. It was superb, brilliant, marvellous. The BBC at last! I was over the moon. It was an extraordinary and wonderful feeling. But the day wasn't over yet.

A few hours later she rang again. I almost had a heart attack, thinking the BBC might have changed its mind. But it was nothing of the kind, Beryl told me. I should've guessed by her exhilaration.

Granada wanted me to write an episode of their thriller series *Shadow Squad*. Would I be available to go to Manchester for a script conference next week? I most certainly would be!

"Two in one day after so long!" She was elated. I was her first drama writer and this was new territory for us both. "They offered three hundred," she said, "but I turned it down . . ."

"Oh, Beryl, " I started to protest, but she interrupted.

"I said it was insulting, so they agreed to four hundred."

I confessed to her I'd have probably done it for two hundred.

"That," she admonished, "is why you have an agent."

It was an incredible day. That night we had a party and drank a toast. "To the bastard at the bank of New South Wales. If he'd lent us money, we might be on our way home by now."

It was the start of many wonderful years. A retreat to Australia was no longer on the agenda. We felt as if we might stay forever.

*****

PART FIVE: THE SIXTIES

Sometimes it was hard to believe the change in our lives between the first two years and the period that followed. After that initial breakthrough it was like a floodgate opening. This was the prelude to the sixties, and I thrived on being there. The BBC bought a six hour thriller, Associated Rediffusion asked me to write episodes of *No Hiding Place* and Granada kept requesting *Shadow Squad* stories. To my surprise, the records show I wrote nineteen of these for Granada in the next few years.

If it sounds an excessive amount, I think the years of radio imposed a rigid discipline. In Australia we worked long hours because of low fees. In *Out of the Bakelite Box*, a book by Jacqueline Kent, I expressed this view. *"We were regarded as people who produced endless yards of words on paper. There were times when, apart from the weekend, we had no social life. All we did was write, write, write our heads off."*

What I found in England was different. There was more time to deliver a script, as well as a more generous fee. So I found myself writing a draft, then, after a few days, analysing and revising as much as possible, trying to improve it to read like a

Peter outside the Wig & Pen Club, London, in the 1960s.

final draft, but never calling it that. It seemed to produce results. After two years Sidney Bernstein, the head of Granada, asked if I'd like to train as a television director. It was tempting, but it meant moving to Manchester, and none of us wanted to leave London. Two years had brought changes. We were comfortable renting a pleasant house in Kensington's Warwick Gardens, and enjoying a circle of friends. Lyn and Perry had survived enough changes, and were now settled into their schools. I came to the conclusion I'd rather write for actors than direct them. Between the variety of offerings I kept writing an occasional play, and amazingly they all sold, some to ITV television, others to the BBC. The sixties was called the most exciting period of British television. I felt very fortunate to be there.

My first television play in October 1960 was the Sunday night Armchair Theatre. By chance it was well publicised, because I'd had a script in a series called *Police Surgeon* screened the previous night. Then, the day after the Armchair Theatre, an episode of *Probation Officer* was shown. Both these and the play were written at different times for quite different companies, but newspapers picked up the rarity of three shows in three days. The television critics made the most of it: *Aussie writer's triple*, or some such headlines. It was sheer chance, but it brought a lot of press coverage.

The play was called *Thunder on the Snowy*. It took place in a migrant work camp with research I gathered before leaving Australia. The research was for a musical about the Snowy River project, where I was to write the script, and composer Bill Lovelock, the music, but it was never made because the finance fell through. Fortunately research like this is rarely wasted. It provided a background for this play, and many years later it also became a location for one of my novels. The play starred Harry H Corbett, a fine actor who went on to make his name in *Steptoe and Son*.

Peter with the cast and director Vivian A Daniels (standing, second from left) on the set of Reunion Day *with cast members including Frank Leighton, Ron Haddrick, Lyn Ashley, Jerold Wells, Reg Lye, Nyree Dawn Porter, Ken Wayne, Alan Tilvern, Patricia Connolly, Ray Barrett, Madge Ryan.*

The next play, *Reunion Day*, was produced by the BBC in 1961. There had been a delay while they arranged to get a mainly Australian cast which included Ray Barrett, Ron Haddrick, Madge Ryan, Reggie Lye and Patricia Connolly. It was midwinter and freezing in Birmingham, but warm and sunny in the studio for a drama set on Anzac Day. Within months of its BBC appearance, Beryl sold the script to a TV network in West Germany. She was quoted in a book about the Agency called *Spike & Co*, that this was her first overseas sale. The Germans paid triple what the BBC had paid, and the same high fee again when they repeated it the following year. My lovely agent learned what a rich market there was for writers outside England, and we all benefited from her foresight.

One country where this play was not shown was Australia, as Frank Packer bought it, then refused to show it because in his opinion it offended returned soldiers. This was dumb and dictatorial Packer at his most irrational. The play, how it was received, and what happened to it, is splendidly described by Susan Lever in a journal article: *Peter Yeldham's Reunion Day: An Anzac Day Play on British Television*.

Producer John Elliott said it was seeing Ray Barrett in this role that led to casting him in *Trouble Shooters*, where he became a star of British TV. We never imagined things like that when we were mates grinding out a living in Sydney radio.

During this fertile period Associated Rediffusion, the London ITV company, produced what I still believe was my best television play. *Stella* was a drama, set in an outback town that was slowly dying as its inhabitants moved away. Stella was the daughter of the hotel owner, a woman in her forties who'd been the belle of the district, facing the prospect of a bleak and empty future. Canadian actress Katherine Blake gave a luminous performance that led to some really wonderful reviews; one Sunday paper described it as a landmark in TV drama. Another called it moving and poetic. It remains a highlight in my life, an ideal cast and a brilliant director. I've always regretted not having a tape of that play starring Kate. At that time tapes were used but then discarded after the shows had gone to air, because everything was still in black and white. TV colour was a few years away, so the networks did not bother to keep what would be out of date recordings. It was a frustration, the number of memorable plays by so many writers, lost after a single performance.

There were proposals to write a stage version of *Stella*. A West End producer was most persuasive, and I wish I'd taken up her offer to fund a production for a tour to test the possibilities, but at the time I was involved in television, as well as being asked to write my first film. Some years after I came back from the UK, *Stella* was sold to an Australian producer. It happened through actresss Wendy Hughes, who was a friend and neighbour at the time. She read the script and her enthusiasm led to its purchase, with her husband as producer. Unfortunately it ended as a disappointing film called *Boundaries Of The Heart*, and was nothing like the British version superbly directed by Peter Moffitt. I was there for most rehearsals of the English production, but not invited to any stage of the Australian version; not at the reading, the rehearsals, or the actual filming. I can't blame Wendy for this. I heard about the problems months later, which showed how writers are sometimes treated by our own nation's film companies.

It was now our sixth year in England, and we felt settled there. Both kids had adapted well to schools, and in 1962 we rented a farmhouse in the Weald of Kent for the school summer holidays. Kent is my favourite part of England, full of history and enriched with hop fields, farms with oust houses, and picturesque towns like Tenterden. We discovered friends galore, actors and writers who lived in the county, and before the summer was over we went looking for a weekend cottage, eventually buying a modest bungalow near the village of Biddenden. It was here Perry learned to ride. A neighbour, Daphne Shadwell kept horses, and he rode every weekend with her from the age of eight.

A strange thing happened, which seemed to illustrate the solid English friendships we'd formed. Dave Freeman came to visit us in Kent, then returned soon after, to buy a farmhouse near us. In the following year friends Peter and Betty Lambda did the same. Peter was renowned for sculpting busts of Olivier and Gielgud, Betty was a star of musicals in London and New York. We met on weekends for long lunches, not yet knowing how deeply this pair would feature in our future life.

In the nineteen sixties the range of offers made it possible to work with producers I admired, on shows that felt challenging. Tony Kearey was that kind of producer, with that sort of show. I first met him when he asked me to work on the very exciting drama series *Probation Officer*. It was a program that pushed the boundaries, and dealt with social problems never before aired on domestic screens.

There are producers who insist writers give them a step-outline, a detailed treatment of everything in the story, at times running to as many as 20 pages. I became notorious for turning down this process, on the grounds that we lose creativity. It feels repetitive, and we're forced to stick to a fixed and agreed framework when writing the screenplay.

Fortunately there are other producers who trust writers and don't insist on this process. Tony was one. I liked working with him as he took risks and had confidence in writers. One script of mine for *Probation Officer* began when I said to him, "I've got an idea. We see a man wake up in a shabby hotel room. He's fully dressed and by the bed is a bunch of flowers. He gradually realises it was his wedding anniversary and he got drunk and went gambling, instead of going home to give his wife the flowers and take her to dinner."

"Sounds interesting," Tony said. "What happens next?"

"Haven't the faintest idea," I said.

"Go away and write it," he suggested. That was Tony, relying on writers to deliver. So I did go away to write it, and it won a British Guild Award. I'll never forget that night. Unlike the Australian guild, there was no short list. Nobody knows what names will be read out. It was a posh affair at the Dorchester, and we were with friends at a table for eight.

"The best drama script," said the announcer, "is *The Gambler* by Peter Yeldham.*"* I thought I was dreaming. Seconds must've passed. I could see the people at our table clapping, then Marge opposite, looking excited, making eye movements that seemed to be saying, *get off your bum and collect it*. Even when I got up and heard the whole place applauding, it still felt as though it was not really happening.

I've been lucky enough to win awards since then, but never has there been the total surprise and pleasure of that one. They were rare, the producers in film or television like Tony Kearey. There was another Tony in Australia, Tony Buckley whom I was to work with, in fact already had done so without realising it, but that comes later.

They are rare those producers. The insecure fraternity want to sit down and discuss each scene, arguing and bending it to their preferred structure. In the end it loses identity as your story, becoming some sort of hybrid compromise between producer, director, and the growing cluster of another opponent, Executive Producers who seem to be rapidly increasing these days.

British television, with features like *Probation Officer* and the single plays, led to films. One day in 1962 Beryl rang to say producer Jon Penington had asked me to write a feature film starring Kenneth More. It was based on a novel by Douglas Hayes, about the world of struggling actors, and its title, an ironic one, was *The Comedy Man*. She negotiated a payment that seemed unreal to me. In fact everything seemed unreal. I'd long ago walked in Sydney streets, gazing at film advertisements on billboards, having hopeful dreams I might write a movie someday, but I never imagined one of England's top actors would star in it.

The story about out of work actors had instant appeal. Having been an out of work writer in London, I knew how empty the days felt, with telephones that never rang, or if they did, it was a wrong number. I knew the make believe of claiming things were looking up, when your pocket was almost empty. It felt a bit like my story as well.

The only problem was the delay in raising finance. I wrote the first draft of the screenplay, then a second draft without a start date. Generally studios declare the script is the cause of any delay, but I was spared this. The lull was caused by two problems. While we all liked it, the subject wasn't a thriller or action movie, not one for the school holidays or the big Odeon circuit. It was a word of mouth movie for a specific audience, in the way some French and Italian films are aimed at special cinemas. The second problem was more personal. Kenneth More had just left his wife after thirty years, to take up with twenty-year-old Angela Douglas. The English public love their stars, but they can be unforgiving, and were in Ken's case. It's the risk of celebrity, and was no help that Angie would play his young girlfriend in the film.

We kept hoping for news, but just before Christmas Day what came like a yuletide gift was a phone call from Hollywood. Robert Day, who'd been first choice to direct *The Comedy Man*, had left because of the delay, and was on the line from Los Angeles. He was about to direct a film that needed a big rewrite, and had put my name forward. Was I available? He explained it was a thriller, gave me a proposed title, but nothing much in the way of detail. Just that it was to start shooting next month in Bangkok. Everything was set, it was all stations go; if I wanted it, I had to be on a plane to Thailand on Boxing Day. There'd be a first class ticket waiting for me at Heathrow, and a contract would be sent to my agent. He and his producer would join me at the hotel in Bangkok.

A Hollywood movie, I thought! Dreams were coming thick and fast. I couldn't contact Beryl who was away for Christmas, but I knew *The Comedy Man* was still delayed, so with the pre-paid ticket and a luxury hotel confirmed, I left a message for her and went to Thailand. I arrived late on Boxing Day, but my luggage went elsewhere. That was bad enough, but at the hotel there was a cable; Bob and the producer were delayed in Tokyo. They would arrive in about three days.

So . . I was the lucky screenwriter without any clean clothes, and at least three empty days to spend waiting for them. I didn't even have a copy of the script. The loss of luggage meant sympathy from the air hostesses who stayed at the same hotel, and by the time the suitcase was located and returned next day, I was on friendly terms with them in the swimming pool. By then they knew I was there to write a film, so in about five minutes I was also their drinking partner. It did no harm that I'd once conceived a radio show called *Air Hostess*!

Then came a rather urgent call from Beryl Vertue. She was back in the office and the contract had arrived. "Did I realise," she said, "that it's a Tarzan film? Jock Mahoney is to play the loincloth hero."

O-Mi-God, I thought, how do I break that news to the nymphets in the pool? *Bloody Tarzan*! They'd drown laughing.

Did I want to continue? Beryl asked. Her main concern was the risk of being unable to finish work on *The Comedy Man*, she explained. That could be at stake if I was stuck in Bangkok, which was possible. Rewrites on location could mean being on the set for weeks. It would be a shame to miss my first film starring Kenneth More in favour of a Tarzan rewrite, she stressed. She didn't need to stress, I could see the dilemma, and the headlines. However I couldn't just leave without making contact, and therefore had to wait and talk to them when they returned.

But it was only Bob who arrived the next day. The producer Sy Weintraub was in Asia, cooking up deals. I liked Bob, and found it difficult to say I felt he'd misled me by just calling it a thriller.

"But it is a thriller," he said. "Action packed, wide screen, good supporting cast. And we start shooting in three weeks."

It was awkward, because he'd been trying to do me a favour. We'd become friends during the drafts of *Comedy Man*. He felt Penington would fail to raise the finance, and this film would be an alternative for me. So we waited for Sy, spending our time seeing local films with English subtitles, and talking of changes that might improve the script, which Bob had brought for me. I grew nervous, for Beryl's call had rung alarm bells. Losing a film with Kenny More and a top cast of British actors would be stupid. "Talk it over with Sy," was Bob's advice.

When Sy at last turned up he was a brisk American, quick to show disappointment that I hadn't done much work on the script. I pointed out I hadn't seen it until Bob's arrival. He promptly pointed out he didn't like the modest changes I'd made.

"Not what I expected. You haven't even attacked the problem," he complained.

"But what is the problem?" I asked, thinking that even a few weeks with Sy was going to feel like a long hard sentence.

"Goddamn it, that should be plain. The story must evolve from the essence." He stared at me, as if to say Hollywood writers would have leapt to the conclusion by now. "The essence," he repeated.

"The essence of—what?" I had to risk it, because I didn't know what the hell he was talking about.

"The essence," he said, "of Tarzan's motivation."

Tarzan's motivation? This tree dweller in a loin cloth's motivation?

That was the moment when I knew Sy and I would never agree on anything. If I stayed I suspected we'd end up seriously disliking each other. So I gave him the changes made to the script— said if he insisted I'd pay back the fare, and booked myself a flight to London.

I got there on New Year's Eve, took a train to Kent where Marge and the kids had gone on Boxing Day. It was freezing cold and snowing—the beginning of the long winter of 1963—when she met me, and we drove back to the cottage through the swirling snow, both of us relieved I'd got there in time. The next day was the start of that winter. We were snowed in, trains and planes were at a standstill; it was lucky I'd got home at all. Within a week came good news, the finance was at last set for *The Comedy Man*, and thankfully I was there to do a few minor rewrites, not handing over to someone else while wrestling with Tarzan's motivation in Thailand.

We started filming a month later. Alvin Rakoff was the new director, and the studio decided it should be shot in black and white. It was a brave decision, probably the correct choice for the subject, an emotional story set in threadbare rooms and back streets that didn't need colour. We filmed in London, and after the main shoot was over, waiting for the editing to finish, Marge had an idea for a short television series starring comedian Hattie Jacques. We wrote it together; a comedy-thriller with Hattie and Bill Kerr, set in Greece and called *Strangers in Paradise*.

Later that year *Comedy Man* had a midnight launch at one of the big cinemas in Leicester Square. To our delight Richard Lane was in London, spending a few days with us, and able to attend. We'd been friends since he helped with my fumbling first radio scripts, and was now President of the Australian Guild, here for an international conference. The reviews were good. In New York it had a big success, and it led to several more films, so I asked Beryl not to accept any television offers for a while. In Australia long after this, I gave a talk about screen writing at the Film and Television School, and was asked to select a favourite movie to show the students. I chose *The Comedy Man*.

It had been a good year that ended in sadness. We were having a meal with friends in Knightsbridge when a shock rumour of John Kennedy's assassination reached London. We simply could not believe it at first, so I went out to the car, and the news was on the radio. After that we sat up till dawn with the friends, Anthony Veitch and his wife, watching the tragic scenes and feeling a personal loss. Somehow Kennedy had felt like a part of our generation, a president with whom we'd identified. I've never forgotten the sadness of that night, and the Alan Jay Lerner lyrics of the song that became a part of the Kennedy legacy: *For one brief shining moment there was Camelot*. An artist friend painted a brilliant portrait of him for us. It hangs on the wall of my study, and has been in every house we've lived in since then.

There were some busy years with film offers after *The Comedy Man* reached the cinemas. Kenneth More had been generous in his praise of the script. Perhaps because of this, the same producer, Jon Penington, asked me to write the screenplay of his next film, *The Liquidator*. It was based on a book by Jon Gardner about a secret agent, a clever spoof on James Bond. There was an amusing contest to get the film rights. Penington read the book on a flight to London. When the plane landed he rang up MGM and bought the screen rights. At the same time an MGM executive was on another plane reading the same book. When his play landed in Los Angeles he rushed to make an offer, to find find Penington had beaten him by an hour. So

MGM decided to be involved and provided finance. This would turn out to be a terrible mistake, but no-one knew it yet.

I began writing, and things moved fast. Just weeks after I finished the script, Jack Cardiff was signed as director. Jack had won several Oscars as a cameraman for films like *Black Narcissus* and *A Matter of life and Death.* There were no delays this time, not with Penington and MGM so keen on the story, and the Metro studio providing the cash. Within months Jack and I were in the South of France, closeted in luxury suites at the Negresco Hotel. Filming was to take place in Nice and along the Cote d'Azur. Trevor Howard and Rod Taylor starred in the main roles. Diana Rigg was proposed for the female lead, but MGM wanted an American, so we ended up with Jill St-John. Diana became a smash hit as Emma Peel in *The Avengers* and would've been wonderful, far better than Jill, but at least we had a stellar cast with half the leading stars of British sit-coms playing key roles. They included my friend Eric Sykes as a hilarious character with his legendary *savoir-faire*.

I went to the Nice airport to meet Rod who I'd known from radio in Sydney. As he arrived he saw me on the terrace and shouted: "Hey Pete, this is a long way from Grace Gibson's fucking studio. Meet the Hoods", he said, as we met. He was now the full Hollywood star; the Hoods were tough characters, his personal trainer and male secretary who, during the film, accompanied him everywhere. Our two lead actors were very different. Rod brash and flamboyant, doing his own dangerous stunts: Trevor, for all his reputation as a hard drinker, a much gentler man. He and I were cricket fans and through it became close friends, in the future spending many days together at Lords, even if we were on opposite sides of the Ashes clashes.

The filming in France went well and there was nothing to warn us of trouble ahead. It had all moved swiftly, with just one surprise. Halfway through the shoot we learned Penington had a partner, Leslie Elliot, a wealthy businessman, and newcomer to films. There was no problem until they had a serious dispute; that was when it turned out Elliot's share was 51 percent of the company, and he swiftly and ruthlessly used it to sack his junior partner. It seemed to happen within hours. Suddenly Jon Penington, the experienced producer who'd hired the unit and all of us, was gone from France. Elliot remained quietly in the background until filming was over. When it was complete he set out to force MGM into a better deal. Rumour abounded there was some fault he'd apparently discovered in the Metro contact. Jack Cardiff and the rest of us felt it would soon be resolved. No sane film producer ever declared war on a major studio. But Elliot was new and didn't abide by custom. He felt he could use the courts to take MGM to the cleaners.

The lawsuits began in December 1965. Elliot first sued MGM in the Hollywood District Court, then in Los Angeles County Court and after that in Britain's High Court. MGM counter-sued Elliot. By this time the film was being called The Litigator.

It was due for release in March 1966, which became impossible. By then it was only released for an audience of lawyers and judges. The delay was harmful. Any postponed film is subject to rumour, and gossip abounded there must be a lot wrong with it. None of us really knew what was taking place, except this bloody man was twisting MGM's tail, and nobody could say if, or when, the film would ever be released. For nine months we had to put up with conjecture over what was causing the delay.

Peace was eventually reached, and apparently Elliot won. The rest of us lost. Particularly poor Jon Penington lost, for I don't think he made another film. The long-delayed 'world premiere' was at the Empire, Leicester Square, nearly a year after its scheduled date. Far too late to maintain public interest. The legal battle had ruined it.

For me there was an additional irony; my contract on *The Liquidator* had required me to write a sequel based on the same character. I completed it in the South of France while we were filming, unaware of what lay ahead. It was called *Amber Nine*, and everyone, including me, felt it was a much better screenplay. I was paid for an initial draft, but after the legal battle nobody wanted any more of the same. So the better script was put away in a bottom drawer until I gave it to Meg Labrum who runs the Australian Film and Sound Archive in Canberra. It remains there to this day.

There was a lot happening in our home life during this time. The children had now adapted completely to living in England. Tenterden in Kent was near our weekender, and had a rural golf course. So rural that sheep also grazed on it when Perry (aged nine) took up golf. He and I played every weekend no matter what the conditions; we were there in fine weather, in the rain, once in snow, and another time had a memorable game on ice, when the course was like a skating link. Our games reawakened my interest and I joined the Stage Golfing Society, open to actors, writers, and anyone in show business. For a mere twelve pounds a year we had memberships of some of the finest courses around London, in places like Richmond Park and Wimbledon.

I took Perry to play at Wimbledon on his holidays from St Paul's school. By then, aged fourteen, he was hitting the ball a long way. On our final hole he hit a shot that he said should reach the 18th green. However it went soaring past there, demolishing the window of the professional's shop many yards behind the green.

They were awfully nice about it. "What a great shot for a kid," the pro said, and told me the window was insured. Luckily people were always amiable when Perry broke windows. This was his third. After the bank in Berkeley Street, there was a window in our flat when he played soccer with his friend Leo Sismanis. We arrived home one night to be told he'd always thought Leo was a better goal keeper. On that day at Wimbledon I had to agree he could hit a golf ball further than I could.

Each year a letter came from Abbotsleigh school, where a prize sustains my mother's memory, asking if our daughter Lyn would be attending. Each time it stressed there was always a place reserved because of her grandmother. And each year I'd written to explain we were still overseas. When she was fourteen I wrote to say it was unlikely we'd be returning to Australia while she was of school age. By then she had adapted with amazing rapidity at her first school, St Mary Abbotts in Kensington, where her initial year's report was full of high marks and lavish praise. It was interesting that such a late starter had done so well. Apart from a few months at Wahroonga prep, aged five, she'd had no schooling until after her seventh birthday. In today's structured childhood that would no doubt be considered deprivation, but she relished the challenge of catching up on those years. When she moved from there to Glendower school, she won a rare prize for being the most popular girl, combined with achievements in scholarship and sport. Marge and I were in the crowd that speech day, bursting with pride. Having been a dunce at school myself, I kept thinking she was truly Faith's grand-daughter.

About this time Spike and Eric Sykes combined to buy a large house near Notting Hill, and Beryl moved the agency there. Writers she represented were soon in residence, and Terry Nation and I had adjoining offices. We had much in common, having both arrived as hopefuls in London, and each surviving a few lean years. Those days were long past for us both. Terry was now writing *Doctor Who* and inventing the Daleks, while I was about to start another film, but we found time to relax.

We set up a game of carpet golf between our offices, and had putting contests in our spare time. Anyone was welcome.

Tony Armstrong-Jones, married to Princess Margaret and hence known as Earl Snowdon, came to visit. He was there to take photos of Spike and other comedy writers for the *Sunday Times*. We assumed he'd arrive in a chauffeured limousine, but were impressed when he turned up alone at the wheel of a Morris mini. He was given a tour of the building and was greatly intrigued by our carpet golf, spending most of his time with us, and taking part in a couple of tournaments. Then out came his camera, and his photos in the next weekend's Sunday Times were not the expected ones of Spike and other comedy lunminaries, but shots of Terry and me putting on our golf course.

Nineteen sixty-three contained good times and bad. It is quite hard to pinpoint exactly when it happened, but our marriage was under stress. We'd been married fourteen years, and perhaps the gloomy predictions of getting hitched too young were coming true, or maybe it was just that old platitude, that after the seven-year itch comes the fourteen-year irritation. Whatever the cause, Marge and I began to find things to quarrel about.

We were still living in Warwick Gardens, and although I had a study and there was heaps of room, I was mainly using the office. I enjoyed the atmosphere there, quite apart from the carpet golf there were other friends like Jonny Speight, Alan Simpson and Ray Galton, always keen to chat. As well, Terry and I worked late, sometimes finishing even later in the local pub, which did not assist the home atmosphere. Things got worse, quarrels blew up one night, and that was when I said it might be best if I moved out while we decided whether we had a future.

I got myself a tiny flat in Park West, where I was torn between relief, and a feeling of enormous guilt. The work on a new film script was going well, but I was dejected, feeling desperate about not seeing the kids. Marge and I rarely met. There was one occasion when we had dinner to discuss my access to Lyn and Perry. It was a favourite Chinese restaurant in Kensington High Street where we were known. She arrived in a new dress, looking lovely. I told her so, a remark she accepted without comment, but then I made a serious mistake by asking "was it expensive?"

She didn't say a word. Just looked at me, picked up her handbag and walked out. And then, as if choreographed for a French farce, the waiter arrived with the food we'd ordered.

"Marjorie, please . . ." I said vainly, but she was gone.

The waiter looked at me; I did my best to shrug, as if this was a game for grown-ups and nothing was amiss—then sat there gazing at the meal. Eating was out of the question, I'd lost my appetite; the only thing to do was pay the bill and leave. Which I did, and could see the waiters gathering to share the gossip as I went.

I thought being unattached after fourteen years would be relaxing, but it mostly wasn't. After a few months I couldn't stand it. So one day I picked up the phone and rang her. Was it possible to meet at a different restaurant for a discussion— and would she promise not to walk out?

There was a longish pause. I sensed a smile when she said it could even be the same restaurant, if I promised not to say anything upsetting. So we met at the same Chinese place. The inscrutable waiters did not blink an eye. So nice to see you both, one said.

I moved back the next day. We spent the rest of our lives together. And they were wonderful years, full of laughs and love. One day when I was writing about a couple who were divorcing and meeting to discuss their circumstances, Marge said: "Use the scene. *Our scene.* She arrives. He says something dopey, and she walks out. Just as the waiter brings the meal."

So I used it, and the cast thought it good fun.

"That surely must've happened to a couple you knew," the actress playing the role said. "It feels quite real."

"Yes, I did know them fairly well," I agreed.

There was a film offer after this from Harry Alan Towers who'd surfaced unexpectedly. An adaptation of the Agatha Christie chestnut renamed *Ten Little Indians*. The cast included Boris Karloff, who rang to ask if I'd visit him to discuss the script. He lived near Harrods, where he disclosed it wasn't talk about the script at all; hearing I was Australian he wanted to talk about the cricket. The Ashes series was about to commence and we spent the afternoon having tea and discussing test matches. All those years he'd lived in America, he'd never lost interest in the game. Because of his health, and currently in a wheel chair, he was unable to take the role, but I remember him and that afternoon with great affection.

Towers was always on a financial tightrope, and most writers had a rule. Give him the script with the left hand and take his cheque with the right. But on this film his cheque bounced and Beryl took instant action, bringing a plaintive phone call from him.

"For Christ sake, get this woman off my back!"

I said innocently, "What's she doing, Harry?"

"You know bloody well what she's doing. She's sending in the fucking heavies to repossess my furniture."

"You mean all those Queen Anne pieces? And the Victorian desk? Surely not the desk," I said, finding it difficult not to laugh.

"It's not funny," he said. "They'll be here tomorrow with a truck."

"Of course they will," I said. "Beryl doesn't make idle threats."

He was at the agency next morning with a certified bank cheque. She rang me with the news. "He has a sense of humour," she said. "He asked if I'd like to invest in his next production."

It was on that film I first met Julie Andrews. She was on her way back from filming in Austria. Our location was near Salzburg and, like her, we were in the first class lounge waiting for flights. A seat in the sharp end was mandatory for writers on their films, a rule enforced by the British Guild. Even Harry had to abide by this. He cannily had a contra deal with Lufthansa, and their planes could always be seen flying in his films, even if they had nothing to do with the story.

Julie was with a few actors I knew, and looked like a fairy-tale princess. She'd been in Austria on location for a new musical, after being passed over for the Eliza Doolittle role she'd made famous in *My Fair Lady*. The actors told me this film would be a smash, it would embarrass the Hollywood casting of Audrey Hepburn as Eliza. They were right. A year later the *Sound of Music* was a massive hit, and most people believe Julie should have starred in both musicals.

By 1965 we'd had several rented homes in the eight years since Spain, and this new move was to a spacious and lovely flat on the top floor of Coleherne Court in Old Brompton Road. It was almost unique, a six-room apartment with two bathrooms and a huge hallway, wide enough for crowded parties, and long enough for games of carpet bowls. The rent, it's hard to believe, was only twelve pounds a week. It came via our friends Peter and Betty Lambda who lived on the same floor, and had a weekender near us in Kent. Hearing the flat was empty they phoned us and we could hardly wait to move in. The vibes were good; just weeks later Beryl said producer Sydney Box wanted me to write the screenplay of his next picture.

Sydney was a doyen of the industry, and it was the first time we'd met. The movie was called *The Long Duel*, a J Arthur Rank film set in India, a conflict between tribal leader (Yul Brynner) and English Police Officer (Trevor Howard). It was August, and we'd rented a house in Portugal for the school holidays, while Beryl negotiated the deal. She cabled me the fee, which enlivened the vacation in Albufeira, our last summer in this idyllic beach town before the travel agents discovered it.

That autumn a tiny group of us, including director Ken Annakin, flew to India to consider locations. We occupied a bizarre hotel in the mountains north of Delhi. It was a huge building, a relic of the Raj when Britain ruled India, and apart from the Indian staff and our tiny advance party of seven, was completely empty. It was chosen to become the accommodation for actors and the crew when we started filming, as well as being the production office.

But the plans went haywire. We spent four frustrating weeks there encountering all kinds of problems that had not been anticipated. Each day seemed to produce setbacks. When new batteries were needed, old batteries had to be exchanged. No old, no new ones. If a river was perfect to film in, it was either dangerous or protected by religious law. To top it, a financial investment promised by a wealthy Maharajah never materialised, so we had to move back to Delhi, contact London and wait for finance from the Rank firm, to pay the expenses. The costly journey to India was abandoned, and the errant Maharajah was never seen again.

A decision was made to film in Spain instead, but new locations had to be found. Ken Annakin was in a hurry; because of this the crew christened him *Pannikin Annakin,* but he was in the process of moving from Britain to tax-friendly Switzerland, and timing is crucial in these sensitive arrangements.

I had lunch with Yul Brynner at Elstree Studios, where he was finishing another film, and he said it was a pity about switching to Spain. He wished we were still going to India. I made him laugh with the horror tales of our stay in the cavernous hotel, hundreds of empty rooms except for our group of seven, and how we sat in a vast echoing dining room the size of a football field, where we were attended by about thirty waiters. At the end of our lunch he'd changed his mind on India. A lucky escape, he agreed. Yul was likable, a pleasant actor to work with, as was Trevor. They were the stars, along with Charlotte Rampling and Harry Andrews.

It had a big gala premiere in London, where the locations in southern Spain were created to look like India. Soon after that I was on a trip back to Australia to discuss a possible Aussie feature film. The producer and I met in Darwin, and flew from there to Adelaide in a Cessna, which was barely the size of a mini, and did not fill either of us with much enthusiasm.

"If we have a crash it'll land safely," said the pilot, which was intended to raise our confidence, but failed to do so. When thirsty we circled airfields, and a truck from town arrived to take us to the pub. In Alice Springs we first heard of problems with the proposed film, and on reaching Adelaide these were confirmed. The project was a non-event due to a lack of finance and some dubious concern about the source material. The producer was upset and I was disappointed, but I'd become philosophic about feature films. It was better to know the bad news, before time was wasted on an unused screenplay. It actually became a chance to spend a few weeks catching up with family and friends. I headed for Sydney, the first visit in ten years.

Because of *The Long Duel* there was publicity. Kay Keavney, once a radio writer, was now a journalist with *Women's Weekly* who organised an interview with me. We spent most of one afternoon, and when it was over we talked about scripts and the lousy amounts we'd once been paid. Inevitably the subject drifted back to *Long Duel*. She asked what fee I was paid for the screenplay. I really didn't want to discuss it, but Kay was an old friend, so I told her after she stressed it would be off the record. Then she asked how long it took I said about three months. It made Kay excited, as the exchange rate at the time was three Aussie dollars to an English pound.

"Hell," she exclaimed, after calculating. "That's forty five grand in just three months.!"

"Plus a month in India, and time in Spain," I said, by now regretting the conversation.

"Even so. Nice if you can get it," she enthused.

"Between us. Off the record, Kay."

"Of course," she promised me.

There were phone calls waiting at the hotel. Both my brothers, old friends like George Richards, actors I'd worked with, and then a name that surprised me. Babe Carter, whom we'd called Auntie Babe, until she asked us to drop the word Auntie, was the Elf's sister, living not far from the same street at Lakemba. As sisters they were contraries, Babe warm and gentle, but frail from a lifetime of ill-health. I'd always been fond of her, but it was the best part of twenty years since I'd seen her, so I went there the next day to make amends. She was very fragile, but sat up in bed and wanted to know all about London and the children, then told me some surprising news. Did I know Elfie had won the opera house lottery about a year ago?

I didn't even know there were lotteries for the new opera house, but was careful with my response. Despite their difference there was a sisterly affection, so I just said it was a surprise, and she'd been lucky.

"Not so lucky," Babe said. "It caused an awful upset. She told the newspapers she didn't know what to do with it."

"That would've brought a few begging letters," I said, hoping she might have given some to her sister, but not wanting to ask.

"It brought heaps of them. Then she started saying she wished she'd never bought a ticket, and didn't want the money. She might give it away. After that was in the newspapers their post box was packed with letters, and someone used a firework basket bomb, and blew it up."

"Poor old box," I said, trying not to grin. "It was blown up once on Empire night when we were kids. I think your sister called the cops." I still hoped Babe had shared in the bonanza, but the way she changed subject prevented me from asking.

"I don't suppose you've been to the house," she said. I shook my head. "I can't blame you. It was never a proper home, was it?"

"Not for me."

"She felt second best, you know. To your real mother, is what I mean. Head girl of the school, so pretty and popular, it was a lot to live up to. But this isn't why I asked you to come and see me. Did you hear your Dad's given up the practice, and he's at Strathfield each day now? I know he'd really like to see you."

"Strathfield? I don't understand, Babe. What's he doing there?"

"Having lunch with Elfie."

"What's happened?" I asked her, so she told me about her sister, who had always been the healthy one.

The Elf was in a private hospital room, and he was talking to her when I got there. Talking, while he sat beside the bed and fed her, then turned to nod at me. "Found it all right then?"

"The taxi driver found it." It was a moment as awkward as our inept few words. He was holding the spoon to feed her; she was gazing vacantly at him, mouth half open, then her eyes stared at me. Nothing moved in her face. No trace of recognition, no words uttered. Nor had there been any, Babe told me, for over six months when she'd gone from decline to a sudden stroke. I watched my father feed her the last spoonful, then tell her I'd arrived, visiting from England. We'll have a short walk, but he'd be back, he promised her.

"Do you think she can hear?" I asked him when we were outside.

"I don't know," he said. "Opinions differ. I feel I have to talk and be companionable. I spend a lot of time here."

He clearly did. Each day this ritual, coming to feed and try to comfort her. I tried not to think about the photos of my mother. "Is it why you gave up medicine?" I asked.

"Of course not. I had skin trouble," he explained. "I had to wear gloves to treat patients. And I was tired. Too many years of night calls."

"I remember hearing the car," I told him. "All hours of the night."

It jolted my memory of those days. There had been three doctors when the war began. Two of them, younger than him had joined the army, so he'd taken over their practices, attended their patients and paid the fees earned to their wives and families. It must have been four long hard years, with day and night calls and queues at his surgery from all the three practices.

We walked and did our best to make conversation. Any flow of dialogue between us was never easy. He didn't mention the lottery win, nor did I raise it. I'd made the assumption this was where it was being spent. Quite soon he said he should go back, as she might miss him.

"I'm glad you didn't get that job," he told me, and before I could ask which job, he said, "the one in the bank."

"Just as well, Dad. They'd have fired me long ago." I smiled, and we shook hands. I would've liked to hug him, but ours had never been that kind of relationship.

It was on this visit I caught up with my brother Dick, having missed his wedding on the way to England. I met his wife Mireille and their three children. I also saw a lot of David, who'd always kept in touch with us. He was now a successful barrister with a growing reputation, and he and his wife, Anne, also had three children. Both brothers and their families came to see me off; it was a time when Sydney airport was smaller and far more friendly. We were able to sit and chat in the open lounge until the first and only flight call, then I could exchange waves with these new nieces and nephews from a window seat in the plane until take-off.

The return trip produced a surprising event. We had a talkative pilot reporting progress from the flight deck, naming the main country towns in New South Wales as we reached them. After that I was trying to doze, but sat up on hearing his announcement we would soon be approaching the Warrego River district in Queensland. Sure enough the river came in sight, then there was a full view of a much enlarged Cunnamulla township, after that the railway, a long straight line that led to Claverton's own siding. Each week I'd ridden across the river to this junction where trains stopped to unload or collect the mail. Finally there was Claverton Downs homestead crystal clear below us, the water tanks, sheds and sheep pens, plus the jackaroo's small room beside the main house, where I supposed some new occupant now lived.

It was amazing, an extraordinary feeling being able to look down at it, trying to reconcile my present different world, remembering back twenty years, to the sixteen-year-old misfit of those days. Whatever possessed me to go there, I wondered, but was unable to find an answer as we left it behind.

Back in London I was sent a copy of the *Australian Women's Weekly* with Kay's article. It was a huge double-page spread in the middle of the magazine with photographs and a dominant headline that leapt out at me: **$45,000 FOR JUST THREE MONTH'S WORK.**

So much for friendly journalists and their promises.

Since the first film for Jon Penington there had been a modest flow of screenplays between television scripts. *Our Man In Marrakech,* was the fourth, starring Tony Randall, fresh from the TV series *The Odd Couple. It weaves a story of suspense, intrigue and comedy, as they are enmeshed in a network of peril and mystery,* said *Kinematograth Weekly.*

I've almost forgotten the peril and mystery, but remember the travel. With the producer and director we flew to Casablanca, then drove across Morocco to Marrakech in search of locations. This was a thriller that began with a murder. Just five minutes from our hotel we found the perfect site for the opening scene. The local market, the *Djemaa el Fna*, was a noisy hubbub of Arab trading. Even more chaos would erupt after finding a murdered man among objects for sale. I went back to the hotel and wrote the first scene. The next few days we found more locations to help fit the story. The following week I was back in London, writing the rest of the screenplay.

There was a lot of travel in the next few years. Not always ending with a film. I spent two weeks in Venice drafting an idea for a movie about Casanova, only to find someone had just finished the same kind of picture on the same subject. I had a wonderful idea for a comedy in Hong Kong that involved the prized British cricket ground, but nobody would allow that sacred turf to be used for a film that made fun of it.

I did spend a great month in Beirut for a film called *Mozambique*. Don't ask why we were filming an African country in the Lebanon. But cinematographers can make the back of beyond look like a Garden of Eden. I really enjoyed Beirut. It was a thriving place; the troubles that destroyed it were not yet apparent. I met a bunch of French-Lebanese students, and spent time with them while they helped to make notes for the screenplay. In years after that I often had postcards from them in Canada, where they had migrated. To me Beirut was a beautiful city: the harbour reminded me of Sydney, but the ambiance was more like a mythical Paris on Sea.

While on the subject of travel, there was one film when I was not invited to view the location, or be present during the shoot, and only saw it after the final cut. It happened just once in England, and ironically was a film made in Queensland.

Norman Lindsay's book *Age Of Consent* was published in 1938 and promptly banned in Australia. We were good at proscribing books in those days. But thirty years later an artist painting a lovely nude girl was acceptable, especially when the girl was eighteen-year-old Helen Mirren. When hearing Michael Powell was to direct, I knew it would happen. But I didn't anticipate being asked to write the screenplay.

I was thrilled, but there were a few surprises. The first, and most comical, was an initial conference we held in fashionable Park Lane with Powell, Helen, James Mason and Mason's celebrated agent, Margaret Johnson. It was meant to take place in her luxury apartment next door to the Dorchester Hotel, but Maggie had lost her keys, so we all sat on the corridor carpet outside her posh front door.

Amid the amusement this caused, there was not much chance for me to ask a crucial question. I'd been hoping James would use his own English voice, which I always felt was his great asset, and not attempt an Australian accent. Over the years there'd been some abysmal accents by imported stars, bringing sighs or sniggers from cinema audiences. But this was hardly a suitable subject to raise for the elite gathering, sitting as if they had chosen to be on the floor outside Maggie's elegant entrance.

The next surprise was on me. Marge and I were having dinner with friends at the actors' club in Mayfair, when Mason spotted me and came to join us. He brought news, the production had the green light and filming would start next month. I asked when we were leaving, which was clearly the wrong question. James looked embarrassed, and so did I, moments later, when it seemed the budget did not include my fare to Queensland. It turned out Micky Powell was inclined to make script changes, and preferred not to have writers on the set.

But at least I felt James and I had resolved the voice problem, when we met the following week in Paris. We were there with

Powell to have final discussions about the script, and I suggested a scene that would make it natural to use his own voice.

It was a brief exchange of dialogue during the titles. A scene when he is leaving his wife. He says he is going home. She replies, "You've been away too long. You don't even *sound like home* any more."

James agreed it would allow him to use his own voice, but along the way to the Queensland coast, he changed his mind. I don't know if it was actor's ego, or Michael's idea for him to play it as an Aussie, but I think the picture suffered. I said as much at a private screening in Soho, when Michael and the Columbia executives showed me the film. At the final credits they asked for comments and I said it was visually stunning, and Helen was a real delight, but I felt Mason's accent was a dud. It sounded phoney and spoilt the film.

"Take no notice of Peter," Mickey told the studio chiefs, "it's the usual writer's neurosis."

They all chuckled, until I said, "There's another detail. I'm afraid you've misspelt my name on the credits." This caused instant dismay. By agreement with the Writers Guild the credits would have be re-done.

There was an interesting aftermath to this film, when I was back in Australia years later. A school friend, Peter Morrison, who had been the publicist on it, gave me his copy of the screenplay. The first three pages were quite different to my pages, but curiously were not part of the finished film. I can only assume Powell decided on a new opening but it had been dropped. Even more surprising was a new name for the role played by Helen. In Norman Lindsay's book she was called Cora, and that was the name on the screenplay. But in the script Peter Morrison gave me, her name was changed to "Ash". I missed this in the version I saw with the Columbia heavies in Soho. It was a very visual film, so perhaps her name was never mentioned. Why Ash, I wonder, and what was wrong with

Cora? In fact, before writing the screenplay my wife painted a picture for me of a girl posing in the sea, and even the painting was always known as "Cora." I sent this second script to join my original at the Film and Sound Archive, with notes about the mystery name change. Cora was good enough for Norman Lindsay. It was good enough for me. I still wonder why it was changed, but never met Powell again to ask him.

It was an exciting life writing feature films. Sometimes disappointing, but mostly exciting. There were premiers, often midnight matinees, big dress-up occasions that ended in the early hours of the morning. There was the thrill, and sometimes pain, of being reviewed in the weekend papers, the *Sunday Times* and *The Observer*. There was something else that happened, which seemed too good to be true.

My agent had another call from Sydney Box. He and his family had been in the film business all their lives. He'd won an Oscar for his screenplay of *The Seventh Veil*, and after that produced many films. Sydney had been ill, but now recovered, and he had a lot of plans for the future. He asked Beryl and me to have lunch with him at The Caprice. Even my agent, used to being wined and dined was intrigued by this invitation.

Over lunch he outlined what he had in mind. Under my contract for *The Liquidator* I'd written the sequel. Sydney felt there was now enough distance between the court cases, so he'd bought the rights of this script *Amber Nine* to be the first of three films. He would be the executive producer of them, and wanted me to be the writer of all three.

The second film was to be an adaptation of Jon Cleary's book *Pulse of Danger*, and the third would be an original by me. But that was just the start. I would be totally involved. On the first I'd be associate producer, and on the second and third I'd officially be producer. I felt astounded, and doubted if I had the experience to produce both films. Sydney assured me I could.

He said he'd been a screenwriter, then a producer; he wanted me to be the same. And I'd have the support of an experienced line producer on each film. Beryl and I left there in a daze. We walked through St James's Park because we wanted to discuss what all this meant. It was a massive commitment, almost too good to be true.

"It's fantastic," she said. Four or five years of work, a three picture deal. "You'll never look back."

As I said, it seemed too good to be true, and unfortunately it was. Two weeks later the contracts were drawn up but not yet signed, when Sydney was taken seriously ill, and it fell to pieces. He was months in hospital, unable to ever work again. Afterwards he and his wife went to live in Western Australia. He died in Perth a few years later.

That was certainly the big disappointment. There were occasional others, reasonably minor in comparison. David Frost, star of *The Week That Was* and *The Frost report* asked me to adapt a book called *Fever Grass*. It was a thriller set in the West Indies, and at the time he was engaged to actress Diahann Carroll, who was to star in the film. I had several meetings with David; we got on extremely well, he liked the script and I was paid handsomely. Then unfortunately he and Miss Carroll parted company, and that was the end of the movie.

I again donated the screenplay to the Film and Sound Archive in Canberra, along with others that were not made. Most of us who write for a living have discards; they are rarely television scripts, almost always the bigger budget movie screenplays. It can happen as simply as Diahann breaking the engagement, or a producer unable to raise finance. I once kept my discards in a bottom drawer until making contact with Meg Labrum, who headed the Archive. Now all my film and television scripts are stored there, as well as these non-events that didn't manage to to see a camera.

They include a Patricia Highsmith novel that Jon Penington wanted to produce, as well as George Johnston's classic novel *Clean Straw for Nothing*. Pat Lovell had the film rights for this book, and she kept always mortgaging her house to raise money for new adaptations, but was never satisfied with anyone's script. She did drive up to Yarramalong to see me one day, claiming she liked my version, but it came to nothing. It was sad, because she had a vision none of us seemed to share, and what could have been a truly memorable film based on a book by one of our greatist writers was never made.

Other occupants of the bottom drawer included a comedy-thriller set in Hong Kong, as well as a screenplay of my own novel *The Murrumbidgee Kid*, and a movie for the Becker Group of Jon Cleary's book *Dark Summer*. Kylie Tennant wanted me to have the rights of her wartime book, *The Joyful Condemned*, and Carl Schultz and I tried to make it as a film, after combining on two successful ABC mini-series. It was a lovely story, and I still have the screenplay, but it was expensive and finance proved to be the problem.

Whatever the payment, and there is usually some payments for them, it never compensates for the wasted time spent on discarded work. It is not a good feeling for a writer if it happens too often. A close friend of mine, a good writer with a fine record, went to Los Angeles, where for years he wrote and was well paid for scripts that, for one reason or another, were never used. It caused depression. Over lunch there one day he spoke of the cruelty that existed in L.A. unless you were a success; how all the former invitations and phone calls seemed to stop. It was unfair, totally destructive and, in the end, made him ill and caused his early death.

Sometimes disappointments come in other ways. I read a fine novel called *A Long Way to Shiloh*, and felt it would make a great movie. One evening there was a call from California, an American producer asking if I'd like to adapt the screenplay. We had an excited discussion, he said he'd contact my agent, while I made notes for the adaptation. I'd long been friends with Ted Willis, president of the Guild, and a few days later we had lunch at the Garrick Club. When writers meet, the first question is—what are you doing? So I asked Ted, who told me he'd just had an American asking him if he'd adapt *A Long Way To Shiloh*.

"Oh shit," I said, and explained the reason why. Over the rest of lunch we discussed the bastardry of producers who behave like this. It was midnight in California, so we rang, waking him, and each told him to get well and truly stuffed. This kind of conduct was annoying but easily forgotten. With major disappointments like the Sydney Box offer, the only thing to do is pick yourself off the floor and start to write something else.

In the late nineteen-sixties, after screenplays for nine films, I'd learned some basic truths about the big screen. *Basic truth One*. Until the script is written the writer is the most important person. After delivery he or she is the least important. *Basic truth Two*. Writers for film have nowhere near the input they have in television. Film is a director's medium, and has been since the rise of the *nouvelle vague* in France. Looking back over what I wrote in the next few years, these feelings must have influenced me, because it was a mixed bag: a new television play for the BBC, then some scripts for America, and just one feature film.

First came the BBC play of the month, then several TV scripts like *Espionage* and the *Zoo Gang*, with John Mills and the lovely Lilli Palmer, both for an American producer. That led to a call from the Mirisch organisation in New York. Would I be interested in a movie they wanted to make in Britain and France? Set in World War Two, a romantic story leading to VE Day. It sounded interesting, the fee was generous, they were enthusiastic, what could go wrong?

The answer was **almost everything**. It became a horror few months. From the start I could not work with the producer assigned to the film. He felt that America alone had won the war; I thought, and tried to tell him, that Britain and a few other countries had also taken part. His ideas and mine were too different to reach agreement. In the end it was close to chaos, an unhappy experience, and a merciful relief when we went our separate ways.

It was the start of winter, which to the surprise of British friends was my favourite time of year. I loved London when the clocks went back, and it was dark by mid-afternoon; what else could you do but stay inside and write? I began to think about a stage play. I'd just turned forty, often contemplating it, but had never tried to write one. First an idea is required, which came about in the oddest way. In the days when women could wear fur coats without being spray painted, I'd bought my wife a mink. It was a secret present for her birthday on Christmas Eve, but winter came early so I'd given it to her in advance. But how did this affect the play I hadn't yet begun to write?

She was wearing the mink on a chilly night when we went to the Ritz in Piccadilly, with our friends Peter and Betty Lambda. After dinner we spent time in the bar, Betty's favourite watering hole when she was in a musical. The waiters all knew her, but seemed to be deferring to Marge, whom they hardly knew at all.

"Could it be the coat," we wondered, and for fun went to another bar where they swapped coats to see what transpired. Sure enough Betty, unknown there, was instantly in the spotlight.

"So what about this," I said. "Two women, they own a mink. They are crooks who rob men trying to get off with them. They move from one city to another, taking turns as a rich lady and her maid or secretary." It was as immediate and simple as that. The next thing was to make this flimsy idea appealing and funny. I suggested a third character. "The first gullible man they rip-off. They swindle him and leave for Paris, but he finds them."

"Why?" Betty asked. " To get his money back?"

"No, to join them," I suddenly sensed it. "He's as big a crook as they are. The three of them form a team. But because they're all so devious, they keep trying to double-cross each other."

"Maybe he fancies one or the other," Marge added.

"Or both," I said, to which we all agreed.

That was how it began, with a mink coat and two great mates, our best-ever neighbours. I finished writing it in March, calling it *Birds On The Wing*, as well as giving myself one big problem. There were too many cities in the play. It had to keep moving because they chased each other from New York, to Paris, then London, Istanbul and finally Tokyo. How were we going to put that on the stage?

Marge and I needed a break and went to the Greek Islands for a brief holiday. On the way back we spent a night at the Hilton hotel in Athens. That was where we heard someone say: "They're all the same, these Hiltons. The only difference is the staff and pictures on the wall."

Bingo! We looked at each other with the same thought in mind. Set the play in an international hotel chain. Have a maid and waiter, with small roles, but flexible actors who could play Americans in the first scene, French in the second, then English, after that Turkish, until they were finally both Japanese for the last scene in Tokyo. It would create expectation, and as they changed nationality to usher in the next country, they could get a few laughs by the brief pursuit of an affair in the style of each country. The pictures on the walls would change from U.S. president to the French head of state, then the Queen, and so on. The set would be the same in each city. Seeing this work on stage a critic praised the set designer for this brilliant idea! But critics and their comments were still a long way off.

Writing the play was the easiest part; trying to get it accepted took far longer. My agent liked it, but it was rejected by several managements. One was Michael Codron, London's top management, which made everyone excited, and then disappointed a fortnight later, as he changed his mind and went off it. While it was being passed around I wrote some television, including *The Persuaders* and an episode of *Van Der Valk*. I'd even started on a new TV play for Armchair Theatre called *Harriet's Back in Town*, when Beryl phoned to say Peter Bridge, a well-known theatrical producer was interested to meet and talk about the stage play. I found out later, he'd only read a few pages and turned it down. My agent prevailed on his assistant to read it. The assistant liked it and suggested Bridge try to find out what happened after page four. As a result of her initiative Beryl had received a call from him agreeing to meet with me. It was a long holiday weekend so she had given him our phone number in Kent, and he would ring on Saturday. We drove to the cottage full of optimism.

Saturday passed without a call. So did Sunday and Monday, the silent phone making it a stressful weekend. We drove back to London convinced Bridge had second thoughts. On the Tuesday he rang; he'd lost our Kent number. I tried to act cool, saying I'd spent the weekend on the golf course. Did he like the play? Yes, he said. He wasn't sure about the title, but he wanted to make an appointment. We settled on Thursday, the following week. Nine more days; it felt like forever.

On the Thursday I woke to the terrible news that Bobby Kennedy had been assassinated. Peter Bridge was also in shock, and we agreed we couldn't discuss a play on a day like this. He said he'd get in touch. I stayed home, watching the sad journey of Kennedy's casket being taken by train across America. At sidings and small towns the crowds of mourners came to grieve; it felt like the tragedy of Dallas all over again.

It was another month before Bridge rang. This time we met. Beryl came with me and we discussed a contract, that would be signed when the details were in place. The problems that followed were complex and long winded. First we had to get the right director, then find the right cast. There is a select group of English actors, not often seen on the screen, mainly stage stars that attract London's West End theatre audiences. One of these was Ian Carmichael, who, after some nervous weeks of indecision, agreed to accept the role. Our director was John Neville, a hugely talented actor whom I secretly thought might play the part better than Ian. The girls could not be cast until Ian actually signed to play the role, and Ian would not sign until he was satisfied they were 'the absolutely right girls'. After weeks of endless discussion about this, those chosen for the first production, were Angela Scoular and Zena Walker, selected by John Neville and, after some more thought, agreed to by Ian Carmichael. I expected to hear we'd soon be rehearsing, but not yet.

The next problem was the title. Bridge now said he hated it. When I protested hate was an extreme word, he said he wasn't sure he really *hated* it, but he didn't like it. His wife hated it. So did his best friend. I sat down the next week writing out alternate titles, most of which everyone hated. Then Mart Crowley, the American who wrote *Boys in the Band*, happened to visit the Peter Bridge office, and saw a copy of my play on his desk. "*Birds on the Wing*. What a great title," he said.

Collapse of the stout party and his hate group. I tore up a list of about thirty substitutions. At last Beryl and I could sign the contract.

New plays invariably tour for some weeks before being judged if they can transfer to a London theatre. Ours was to be a long tour, at Carmichael's own request. After more than a year of hassle and losing hope, rehearsals began at the Irish Club in Belgravia.

We opened in Edinburgh to an enthusiastic audience. I'll never forget that opening, and the joyous sound of hearing full-bodied laughter from a packed theatre. There is nothing quite like it. We toured for six weeks in English towns, then flew the whole show, the sets, cast, director and writer, to Toronto in Canada, for a three week season in the vast O'Keefe Centre. There, on hearing it was our wedding anniversary, Peter Bridge flew Marge first class to Canada. It was a generous and kind thought. She was able to share the excitement of these weeks in this massive theatre. It seated over a thousand people and we filled it every night, making our bank managers happy, yet it was towards the closing week in Toronto, with full houses and dollars pouring in, that Carmichael began to feel uneasy about the prospect of a London opening.

A known neurotic, Ian's last appearance in the West End had been in a show that failed, and he knew another failure would harm him. He was the star, the name above the title, so if the show flopped he would be held to blame. When we returned to England and resumed the last section of the tour in Birmingham, he was uneasy and nervous. He started to invite friends to come and take a hard and critical look at the play. Matinees were the worst; the front stalls seemed to be full of Carmichael friends armed with notebooks, as well making copious audible comments. The actors were soon upset by this. We all became uncomfortably aware of a looming crisis. His various director friends said the direction was at fault and each was prepared to take over, which annoyed John Neville. Writers visited to say they could easily improve the play with a rewrite, which upset me. The actors grew depressed by these undercurrents, and their performances suffered.

It was a harmful atmosphere and the play was badly damaged by it. I got furious, telling Bridge the tour had been much too long; we should close the show and get rid of Ian, unless he stopped white-anting everyone with his phobic behaviour. It was correct, the tour had been long. Most plays tour for about five weeks; I pointed out there would have never been problems if we'd moved to London then. Whereas our tour including Canada was already twelve weeks, with another three to come, and Ian's insecurity was getting worse. As it increased and the end of the tour approached, I put Bridge in a situation where he had to get a commitment from Ian or get rid of him.

The theatrical world is the only place where a playwright has this mandate. It became a Mexican stand-off. Bridge believed in the star system and was desperate to keep Carmichael. Ian was now convinced the show was failing; he did not mince words. It should have serious rewrites and a new director. I was feeling my own anxiety, being sent notes by everyone concerned, including Carmichael's friends, telling me what was wrong with the play and, in their opinion, how to fix it. After our big success in Canada, the months that followed became traumatic. I could not focus on anything. I was irritable and difficult. My wife was patience personified, but she knew word was spreading through the industry and wounding us. We all realised it was harming any future prospect of the play, upsetting the actors who had to be on stage with Ian, and hurting me, having to endure this increasing debacle.

A week before the tour ended Ian wrote me a polite note, saying he felt unable to continue and wishing me the best. I was dismayed that our high hopes had ended so badly yet felt relief this cloud he'd engendered was over. It was a sad final night, everyone still hoping we could salvage the play and start again, but no-one believing it.

That was in April of 1969. Four months later I had a phone call from Peter Bridge, asking me how I felt about Bruce Forsyth playing the lead role? I thought it was a fairly weird idea, but took refuge by saying I'd think about it. Bruce was known for *Sunday Night at the London Palladium*. He was immensely popular, and had starred in a musical play by Neil Simon, and co-starred with Julie Andrews in a recent film. Julie spoke well of him so I agreed to meet, and instantly liked him. Then an American who'd directed Bruce in the Simon play *Little Me* turned up, and things began to fall into place.

After casting Julia Lockwood and June Barry we were suddenly back in business. Sadly John Neville had departed to start his own theatre company, but our new director Harvey Medlinsky was enthusiastic. We had an eager cast— best of all, we had a happy company without the shadow of a neurotic star.

The play opened in Liverpool, with a truly appreciative audience, and a celebration afterwards. It was there that someone spoke the fatal words. "A smash! It'll run for years in London." Word of its success and a great review in *The Stage* prompted a call from American producer, George Abbott. He wanted to book the play for Broadway, and was coming to see the third week at Coventry.

Unfortunately the enthusiasm of the first weeks did not extend to Coventry. We were in a barn-like theatre where a wide orchestra pit meant the audience was too distant from the stage, creating what felt like a cavity between actors and audience. It certainly affected our cast. Lines that had previously raised laughs landed with a dull thud in Coventry. All week it was like that, and concern had caused complaints before the end of the week. By Saturday night, with Abbott out front, it was a dispirited cast who gave a dreadful performance. After it I was confronted by an angry American, who felt his precious time had been wasted.

"If you imagine I'm gonna to put this fucking thing on in New York, you must be crazy," was his parting sally, as he got into his hired limousine and was driven away. I went back to London with June Barry and her husband. He drove; June and I sat in the back seat, drowning our sorrows with a bottle of wine, thinking of what might have been. Fortunately there were no more venues like Coventry, so morale picked up. After a six week tour we opened in London at the Piccadilly Theatre in October, 1969.

My agent Beryl had always felt it would make a good film, and spoke to Harry Saltzman, co-producer of the Bond series, suggesting Michael Caine for the lead. Mike came to see the matinee on the Saturday before opening night, and liked it enough to say he was interested in the role. Saltzman had other plans, persuading everyone to wait for the first night reviews.

It was a packed house, a good audience, but the London critics were mixed. Some enthused, others were accustomed to Bruce in variety shows, and didn't rate him. It was enough to dismantle the film deal. Saltzman backed out, offering Caine another movie role. It was a disappointment. Mike was the flavour of the year and would've been terrific.

The play ran for just over four months at the Piccadilly, which was not what we'd hoped for. The theatre is tucked away in Denham Street, a venue without the passing trade of Shaftesbury Avenue. It needs special word of mouth to get a long run there, and this was not a long run. I could feel the concern backstage; during the Christmas period the play barely covered costs, and I took a royalty cut. When it closed at the end of February 1970, I felt the two and a half years of work, the struggle to revive it, the battles with Ian, and the months of stress had been almost for nothing. It was a cold and wet winter the week it ended, and even though it had reached the West End, I considered it a failure.

It was about this time I reluctantly changed agents. Beryl Vertue joined the Robert Stigwood Organisation to become a film and television producer, a career that has been a dazzling success for her ever since. We parted on the best of terms and remain close friends to this day. She suggested I speak to Harvey Unna, an agent whose special interest was theatre and stage plays.

In fact Harvey had already received an enquiry from a German production group about staging *Birds on the Wing*. So I joined him as a client. The play was sold to Germany for a season in Berlin's *Komodie* Theatre. Although invited, I thanked them but did not to attend the first night. I'd had enough. But a few days after the opening Harvey rang me; he'd received the reviews and being fluent in German had assessed them. He said they were good, and posted translations to me. They were better than good, they were fantastic.

It ran with full houses in Berlin. Their usual season for a stage play was three months. *Auf Und Davon* as it was called, because the English title didn't translate, ran for six months. A play that was scheduled to replace it flopped, so they brought *Birds* back again with the original cast. It kept running with enthusiastic full houses. I went to its first anniversary in West Berlin the following year, spending a week there, being treated like a prince. I got to know the actors, and explored West Berlin with the two brothers who owned the theatre. They planned to renovate it, and asked me to write a new play for them, one that would open the restored *Komodie* the following year. It would be a gala event attended by the German Chancellor.

Meanwhile *Birds* ran in Berlin for a record second year, then had a long tour all over Europe with that same original cast. It was also bought by the BBC as a series starring Richard Briers and Julia Lockwood. By that time a French version had begun in a Paris theatre, and ran for a year. In 1972 it was nominated as the top-grossing play in Europe.

It had been a traumatic eighteen months getting it on the stage, but it became an astonishing success. It never made Broadway or the big screen with Mike Caine, but it kept being produced in theatres around the world. Twenty years later my wife and I went to an opening night of a new version of it in Hamburg. Just last year, when writing this, my Munich agent sent word of a *renaissance* with more productions, so its life has now extended to fifty years. It has played in America and most countries of Europe, and in the years since I wrote it, has earned more than anything I've ever written. But apart from the financial reward, I experienced great pleasure at the way it proved to be a favourite in so many countries. I also had a letter from Ian Carmichael expressing his satisfaction at the success, and admitting he made a mistake in giving up the role. I think it would've had a longer run in London with Ian, but in my opinion the best actor in that main role was Claus Biederstaedt, who played it in Berlin as well as many other cities, then went on to star in my next play, the role of a neurotic dentist that I'd written for him. The play in which our leading lady unfortunately and accidentally stopped the show!!

The new play, *Ready When You Are, Darling*, was to be the gala opening at the same theatre, now refurbished in West Berlin. The German President, the Mayor of the city and various dignitaries were to be guests. It was a considerable honour. But disaster struck and the gala night performance had to be cancelled.

In our final dress rehearsal the leading actress fell and broke her arm, ending up in hospital. A few days later she bravely played the role with her arm in plaster and a sling, but by then the President and his flock had moved on to other engagements. I sat up all night with the cast, drinking Berlin's famous white beer in a cellar bar, while waiting for morning papers with the reviews. As expected, they were not as good as *Birds* had been. It had a routine season, and a short tour in England. But you win some and lose some; writing for the theatre was like that. With a neurotic leading actor and an unlucky leading lady, it was never dull.

During much of this time we lived in Coleherne Court, South Kensington. It was a place where good things happened. Both kids were doing well at school. Marge was painting, and had begun to experiment with stained glass lampshade, and I'd hardly stopped writing for films or television. It was in this apartment, and our previous house in Warwick Gardens, that we felt fully assimilated in London and the British way of life.

We had made several trips to Australia, but never considered a permanent return.

I loved this part of London, loved the busy streets and close proximity of friends, relished the book shop opposite, and the Italian restaurant five minutes away. But we did think it would be nice to own something substantial for weekends and holidays instead of our Kent bungalow. We tried to buy a 16th century farmhouse with several oast houses and a moat, but a surveyor gave it such a shocking report that we got cold feet and didn't go ahead. He said the moat would flood, the oast houses were fragile, and the main house was slowly being eaten by woodworm and may collapse. We often wonder if the surveyor now owns it, because after fifty years the house he so thoroughly doomed is still in fine shape. No sign of any floods or woodworm. My son and daughter-in-law passed it on a trip to England last year, and reported it is standing firm and looking lovely.

It did start Marge on a search for somewhere else. She spent weeks driving to prospects in Surrey, Sussex and Hampshire without success, and was on the verge of giving up. Then one afternoon she came home with news. "It's not exactly a weekend cottage," she said. "Not a cottage at all, but you might as well have a look at it."

"Where is it," I asked.

"Not far," she replied. "You may hate it, but ten acres and being only a half hour from London is probably worth a look."

"How can it have ten acres and be just a half hour from London?"

"Ah well," she shrugged. "The owner's name is Gowring, and he's Scottish," which felt like an odd and unnecessary change of subject.

"What's he like?"

"Funny."

"Comical?"

"No."

"Funny peculiar?" She nodded with a smile. I was getting curious, so I asked, "When can we see it?"

"If you really want to . . .now if you like."

So we drove out of London, down the A3 towards Epsom. The light was fading when we reached the village of Ashtead. This seemed to be a dormitory suburb with clustered houses, not a bit like the fertile fields of England. No ten acre blocks here. But then we drove over a railway crossing and into a rural area. Open fields, a few houses, signs of sheep and cattle grazing.

"This seems better," I said, but it was growing dark.

"You won't like it." She was making me more curious with each passing minute. We drove along a country lane. Ahead was the outline of a structure, like something in a Bronte novel. Or a horror movie.

"Is that it?" I asked.

"Worse than that," was the answer.

By now we'd lost the battle against the light. There was the shape of a house far off the road, but it was too dark to gauge its prospects.

"It looks as if it has some land," I said.

"Yes, darling, I told you, ten acres. But the house . . .! "

"What's wrong with it?"

"Everything." There was a pause. "Well, almost everything."

"Seems to be lots of trees. Are they oak trees?"

"Yes, darling. That's why it's called *The Oaks*."

"Nice name."

"I'm afraid it's too late to see anything now," she said.

"Then let's come back tomorrow," I suggested. "If it's as horrible as you say, maybe we can do something with it."

"Like driving past and forgetting it," she suggested.

We drove back after breakfast the next day. I could hardly eat any breakfast. The way my wife was behaving made me curious and eager to see it. We went through the village again that didn't look any better in full daylight, then over the rail crossing to the rural road and a feel of genuine countryside. After that we turned into a driveway, a surprisingly long one, to be confronted by a shabby Edwardian house that seemed to have been painted in grey undercoat. I expected it to be a ruin by the details I'd been given, but it seemed substantial. Two stories, a third floor with attic windows below a slate roof. "So what's wrong with that?" I asked.

I was advised by Marge to look inside. We met Mr Gowring, a former engineer on the Forth Bridge, which explained the sombre grey paint. We went into his kitchen which was an alarming place, with a live gas jet protruding from a wall, its flame surely capable of setting anyone standing close to it on fire. There was a primitive scullery sink and an Aga stove that didn't work, as we found out later.

From there we proceeded to a huge room that looked like the local tip. It was filled with motorbike parts, oilcans, spare tyres, a vast litter of tools and what the English call rummage, which often means junk that defies any other description. It was the workshop from hell, and not a pretty sight.

"The living room," Marge said, maintaining a poker face.

"Right." I tried to match her in this contest of impassivity.

We moved on. An untidy room with a fireplace was surprisingly free of any garbage. Then a room with sawdust on the floor and lots of carpentry tools, which I was told had once been called the dining room.

After that we went upstairs. There was nothing too awful about the bedrooms apart from shabby wallpaper and a smell of gas. The attic was four rooms, with kitchen and bathroom, clearly unused, but an ideal nest for Lyn, I thought. This might keep her at home, because at twenty, she was more interested in London life and boyfriends.

From there we went outside. Behind the house was a woodland which ensured privacy. The first surprise was a large area of smooth green grass. "Tennis courts," I said.

'The Oaks', Ashtead Woods, Kent.

"One's a croquet lawn," she murmured, leading the way to an apple orchard then a vegetable garden and an impressive glass house.

"Not bad," I commented. It was a rather massive glass house.

"Keep walking," she said.

"What else is there to see?"

I suddenly realised she was pointing to her real objective.

"Holy shit," I said. "Stables!" And there they were. Four stables, a yard and a hay loft. Precisely what our son had hoped for all his life. "Bloody stables!" I turned to where she was smiling.

"You conned me. I love the place."

"So do I. It's as tatty as hell, but we can fix that."

We decided not to bargain. The price was twenty thousand pounds, and the eccentric Mr Gowring added five pounds to the price for a load of coal that had just been delivered. We happily agreed. Driving home I asked Marge why she'd decided on this astute entrapment.

"Because you never wanted to own property. You said we had such a lovely flat at an amazing low rent, we'd be mad to own a house."

"How could I have said anything so stupid?" I protested, thinking fondly of the acres, the tennis court and the stables.

"You said it often," she replied with a smile.

Two months later our furniture was being loaded when there was a call from our solicitor, Bill Balmer. "We've got trouble," he announced.

"Bill, our furniture is on the footpath, and rain is forecast. What kind of possible trouble? Everything's been paid."

"Not quite," Bill said. "You haven't paid for the coal."

The coal. I'd forgotten the bloody coal.

"Bill, can you give him a fiver."

"He says it's a breach of faith, and wants you to pay in person. He won't hand over the keys until you do. He's a bit on the odd side. It's become a matter of principle."

"Tell him, stuff the principle. We're not going to make legal history going to court over five quid and a bunker of coal."

In the end sanity prevailed. Gowring got his five pounds, and we moved in that afternoon. It was springtime, and there was a canopy of oak trees over the long winding driveway. It was Perry's first sight of the house. He had just turned fifteen, and been riding at weekends in Kent for half his life. Once we told him about the house we'd promised to buy him a horse. Thrilled by the stables and forest behind our house with riding trails, he also noticed the fine home of our neighbour who owned seventy acres containing both cattle and horses. He went next door, as he told us later, to introduce himself. The door was opened by a housekeeper.

"Excuse me." he said, "my name's Perry Yeldham and we've just moved to The Oaks. I came to say hello to the owner of the house."

"One moment," she replied. "I'll see if His Lordship is available."

O-Mi-God, Perry thought, *a Lordship. What've I let myself in for?* She returned, taking him to meet an elderly man who smiled and shook hands. "I'm Barnby," he said.

"I'm Perry," was the only answer to that.

They talked for an hour. Lord Barnby was a charming hereditary peer who rode daily. When we bought Perry a horse, our son and his ninety-year-old friend rode together at weekends and school holidays.

Meanwhile we had problems to sort out. The local company was called to fix the gas leak. The jovial inspector roared with laughter.

"You ain't got one leak," he said, "you got thirty of the bleeders!"

The Aga stove, supposed to cook meals and provide hot water, failed to do either. There was no hope of a hot shower, or a roast dinner. The Aga couldn't stay alight long enough to boil an egg. Marge hated it, and set about transforming the kitchen. A new sink, new stove and a hot water system. When this was done our kids had the astonishing sight of their mum—by nature tranquil—smashing the Aga stove to pieces. By the time this was done she was exhausted but content, and came inside to enjoy a large gin and tonic.

Friends came to see the new house and named it 'Yeldham's folly'.

Why, they wondered, did we leave London to bury ourselves in the countryside? We told them it was hardly countryside, being only thirty minutes from Waterloo station. Which, incredibly, it was.

When I wrote a new play for Armchair Theatre, I didn't expect it to become a television serial, and didn't particularly want to write it. The play was called *Harriet's Back in Town* about a divorced woman finding life is better after the breakup. The serial was a new project for Thames Television who suggested they wanted to star Pauline Yates. I knew she would be perfect for the role, so I was talked into writing the first few scripts, and editing others during the year it was on air. I didn't tell them, but the play had been written with Pauline in mind. She and her husband Donald Churchill were our close friends, and this came at an interesting time. Donald and I had just decided to rent a room in Chelsea, to try collaborating on a new stage play. The result was a comedy we called *Fringe Benefits*, which starred Ronnie Corbett on its tour, and six months later moved into the West End with Brian Rix and a top cast at the Whitehall Theatre. After that it had a good run in Berlin, and an even better one at the Saint Martin theatre in Paris, where it played for two years, was shown on television, and made us decide to write another play together, as soon as we had another idea.

Meanwhile our 'folly' underwent a gradual transformation. We found a handyman who painted the outside; the sombre grey of the Forth Bridge became a gentle shade of white. Summer was coming, so we built a barbecue. Marge laid a new parquet floor to obscure the oil spills in the dining room. After that we cleaned out the dreadful clutter in the living room and put down carpet; it was amazing how elegant the large room became with bookcases and a new fireplace, followed by furniture and a baby grand piano. It was transformed. If the Scot could see his workshop, he'd think he was in the wrong house.

Next task was upstairs with its flaking wallpaper. We made a house rule. No-one went past without stripping a chunk of paper off the wall. In the mornings you didn't get breakfast without the evidence of a successful rip off, and when guests stayed they were briefed on the wallpaper rule. It became a contest to remove the longest strip, and soon the bare walls were ready to be redecorated.

We did a great deal of the repair work ourselves. The hardware shop in the village could not believe their luck; we became their new best friends. It took about nine months solid work, painting and decorating. Fortunately at this time *Birds on the Wing* was flying high in Europe, and royalties were coming in to pay the bills.

The following year land and house prices skyrocketed. Lyn's new boyfriend, Rod Cawthorne, was in real estate, and he estimated the place was now worth five times what we'd paid. But we had no plans to benefit; we bought it because Marge said it was what she'd been hoping to find for years, a truly lovely home to live in. It was a pity we found it so late. It would've been a perfect house for the children to spend early years, and grow up there. Lyn took the attic rooms as her flat, but after she met Rod she was more often in London. Perry got some good years out of it, especially after he left St Paul's school and decided his future was with racehorses. He went to work for John Sutcliffe, a trainer in Epsom, and he even rode as an amateur in the winter hurdle races. Sutcliffe also trained the ex-racehorse we'd bought for Perry, who turned out to be a surprise. Not ex at all, but an eager hurdler. In return we took some of his horses to spell in our field, among them Specify, winner of the 1971 Grand National.

Marge and I got caught up in this horse fever. We not only went to Ascot and courses all over England to see Perry ride, but found ourselves on winter mornings helping to feed any canine guests in the stables. These were often full; Perry, barely out of school, turned entrepreneur, buying horses and selling them to trainers from Malta and Cyprus.

One Sunday John Sutcliffe came to visit, asking how we were coping with that "ferocious beast". He meant Specify, who at times had escaped from his stable, run wild, and stopped the traffic in the streets of Epsom.

"What ferocious beast?" Marge smiled. She went to one of the fences to call "Specie darling." Specify promptly cantered up to greet her and she gave him a kiss. An open-mouth Sutcliffe could hardly believe it.

She had a rare kinship with animals, and we'd had a wide variety of them. First a cat called Cleopatra who perched on my desk to watch me type radio scripts. Cleo sat on all the finished pages, not objecting to being lifted each time I added a new one. We had a cocker spaniel in Wahroonga, and a boxer dog in London. In Ashtead my wife and daughter went to buy a small sweet puppy. This turned out to be a rash move. They arrived home with what they thought looked small and sweet, but his feet were enormous. We christened him Claude, and he rapidly grew—then grew even more, like all bloodhounds do. At meal times I could feel his hot breath as he peered over my shoulder to see what was on the plate.

"Sit down, Claude," I'd say.

"Dad, he is sitting down," Lyn and Perry would reply in chorus.

Bloodhounds not only grow fast, they follow scents. Before long he was in pursuit of trails all over southern England. We lived in Surrey, but his nose took him to Hampshire and Sussex, from where we'd get phone calls: "We have your gorgeous dog and will keep him safe till you collect him." In vain Marge said if they didn't feed him he'd find his way home. No, they'd reply, he's too precious for that. So off she went to bring Claude home, where he'd flop down to rest before setting off on another journey.

To control his roving we sent him to obedience school. He made friends with Jason, a Labrador whose owner was ill, so we inherited both dogs. The school promised he'd be a calming influence. The next day Claude disproved this by a marathon run, almost reaching Brighton.

Some weeks later Marge was driving home, when she saw the back view of the village policeman who appeared to have Claude on a leash.

"Oh thank you. That's my dog," she said, pulling up alongside him.

"Oh, is it, Madam?" The copper turned to face her. He was covered in slime from the local duck pond, and so was Claude, wagging his tail in cheerful recognition. Trying to retrieve him the cop had fallen in, and a bunch of school kids had laughed at the sight. The law was seriously displeased; he threatened any more trouble, and Claude could face a very large fine and a short future.

That night we held a high level conference on his future. It was apparent there was no way we could confine him to Surrey. Soon he'd be on his way to Devon, after that Cornwall or Wales. Or perhaps he'd take the alternate route, head north and aim for Scotland. A heart-breaking decision was reached after several gin and tonics. Claude had to go. We took him back to the breeder where we'd bought him, and she found him a new owner in Kansas. We never forgot him, and liked to think of him at full stretch across the prairies, headed for the next state, or perhaps on his way to Canada.

During this time Perry rode his own horse called Amundsen in hurdle races all over England. He rode as an amateur, and in winter when the races were either hurdles or steeplechases, most riders were amateurs. Among them was John Oaksey, a journalist for the *London Telegraph*. At one meeting he rode a mount called Great Scot, and in ferocious weather was beaten in a tight finish by our horse. Hence a lead story in the next day's newspaper: *Amundsen beats Scot. History repeated itself at Canterbury racecourse yesterday, when in driving sleet Amundsen brilliantly ridden by young Perry Yeldham, beat Great Scot to The Pole once again.*

We had some wonderful years at The Oaks. I loved the mix of writing in a peaceful study that overlooked the paddocks, while able to have so many other interests. At the same time things were stirring in Oz. First I was offered a film, then the head of drama at the ABC, John Cameron, bough a miniseries of mine called *Run From The Morning*.

The title was a suggestion by Tony Morphett, whom I met for the first time on another brief visit to Australia. We had a long boozy lunch with Glyn Davis, a former policeman in England who I'd known when he'd retired from the force and provided story lines for crime shows like *Shadow Squad* at Granada.

I was leaving for London that afternoon, but there was lots of time. It was a BYO restaurant and Tony arrived with four bottles of wine.

"My God, " I said.

"Just in case," Tony answered. "I can always take some home."

He didn't, of course. We settled down to mutual interests, while making short work of the wine. By three o'clock lunch was proceeding cordially; at four o'clock the last bottle was empty, time was short, and an urgent taxi was required. I arrived at the airport perilously close to departure time, and woke up at our first stop in Bombay with a hangover.

Time, although we didn't yet realise it, was running out for our lovely life at The Oaks. Apart from writing, and planning another stage play with Donald Churchill, there was this other existence; the horses, the tennis court, ferocious games of croquet, plus lots of weekend barbecues, and the sheer joy of living in such a graceful house, the best we'd known. Marge had turned the place back to its glory days, retrieved its style that existed before the Firth of Forth engineer had put his eccentric imprint on it. We intended to be there for years. But nothing stands still, hence the regret we hadn't found it when the kids were younger.

In December 1972 Lyn married Rod Cawthorne, with a reception at the Hyde Park hotel in Knightsbridge. Two years later, after the birth of their first child, they decided to move to Canada. In the same year, at the age of eighteen, Perry had an urge to see the land of his birth. As he said, we'd taken him away when he was two, so he had no idea what Australia even looked like. He then cleverly got a job on an aircraft transporting horses, going via New York to Sydney.

A few weeks later we received an excited phone call saying: "I love this place. I can't imagine why you left." He came back to spend Christmas with us, then returned to settle in Sydney. Which left us roaming around in a house too big for us any longer, echoing with the memory of good times and departed children.

Because of the work being offered, and the excitement of what was happening in Australia, we gradually decided on a new design for living. We'd spend half the year in Britain, half in

Australia. We could also fly via Canada when Lyn and Rod moved there. He was currently in Vancouver looking for a house. Lyn and Philip, their one year old, were soon to follow.

Having made our decision, it was clearly impossible to live part time at The Oaks. So we reluctantly put it up for sale. It had been a place of such good memories. But one particular recollection still lingers, and always will. Looking out from my study window one day, I saw our daughter and son engaged in a debate. They were deep in conversation, and I wondered what was causing such a serious discussion. We found out on our 25th wedding anniversary. The place was full of friends who'd come to share our celebration, and that was when the pair of them presented us with a gift they'd saved up to buy. It was a silver tea set with the inscription: *Marjorie and Peter, 27 October, 1973.*

It came as a complete surprise and, without doubt, the nicest present in our lives. Since that day it has accompanied all our moves, and is still in a nearby cabinet as I write this. It was a simply wonderful gesture that Marge and I never forgot. Even now I can still remember watching them from my study window, wondering, but never guessing the surprise they were planning.

*****

PART SIX: AFTER THE OAKS

It was the year when rich Arabs were flushed with wealth from oilfields, and paying crazy prices for English property. We waited vainly for one to appear up our driveway, but they were more interested in the glamour pads of Hampstead or Knightsbridge. In fact we weren't rushing a sale. On more optimistic days we discussed whether we could change plans, buy a flat for shorter spells in Sydney, and keep the Ashtead house. But in the end we realised it was impractical; we needed a house in England we could lock up or rent when we were away. Soon after there was an offer from an American couple, so we agreed to sell and buy something more compact. It also solved a problem with the animals, as the American buyers agreed to take Chloe the cat, and Jason, the Labrador.

It was awful leaving them, in particular the cat, for she knew. Lyn and I were waiting while our furniture was loaded, when Chloe darted aboard the removal van and buried herself deep into the furniture. It took ages to retrieve her, they had to unload most of the van while Jason gazed at us with his mournful labrador eyes. Lyn and I drove away from there when it was over, feeling heartbroken and guilty.

We temporarily moved into a flat while the furniture was stored, then found a perfect house alongside Richmond Park, and agreed to buy it, until we were "gazumped." A horrible word for an unsavoury practice. After accepting our offer, the agent rang to say the owners had received a better offer. Did we wish to compete and go higher. We said no, it had been for sale, not for auction. It was Lyn, prior to leaving for Canada, who actually found the answer, a brand new house in a quiet street off Kingston Hill. This was ideal, exactly what we needed, compact with sufficient rooms and a very small garden. We could rent it in the English winter, and migrate to Australia's sunshine. This was to be the new way of life, in Surrey and Sydney. No winters, just perennial summer.

It was the summer of 1975 when we were next in Sydney for Perry's 21st birthday. The next week he saw an advertisement for a cadet journalist at the *Inverell Times*, and wrote to apply. It was a bad time for youth employment, but he had a battered old car and, unknown to us, drove to Inverell to follow up his application. The editor, impressed by this initiative, disposed of about twenty hopeful letters and gave him the job. He worked in newspapers for the next 40 years; first Armidale, then Dubbo where he became sports editor, then moved to AAP and after that the *Courier Mail* in Queensland. It was there in Brisbane he met Mary Anne McDonald, falling in love before he learned she was the boss's daughter. Her father was the CEO of Queensland newspapers. Perhaps concerned by possible accusations of nepotism, he headed to Sydney and a new job, this time with Fairfax. It was a very happy day for us when Mary Anne arrived to join him. A year later they were married, moving to Collaroy, the third generation to live there, and producing four fine children who are now adults. Some of these adults are now adding to the size of Christmas parties by producing children of their own.

That summer we went to Melbourne to see Marie Trevor, a friend of many years, and at lunch met Tom Hegarty. Tom was a top writer with Hector Crawford, and adapted *A Town Like Alice* with English writer Rosemary Anne Sisson. It was a brilliant show, an award winning script with fine performances. Along with good films like *Caddie* and *The Devil's Playground* we were excited at the quality of all we saw in the cinemas and on television. By then, as part of the plan to live in both countries, we'd bought a flat in an apartment block at Collaroy before returning to England.

In the house on Kingston Hill I started work on a new play with Donald Churchill. It was based on a comedy idea we'd had in mind for some time. The plot was simple: some high earners trying to reduce their income tax invent a fictitious character, a female public relations expert and claim her as an expense on their tax return. Trouble occurs as dozens of others hear about it and they also employ this fictional lady. She becomes a high earner, the highest in Britain, and disaster looms when the department of Inland Revenue realise she is *not paying any tax. Had in fact never paid tax. So they go looking for her, the richest woman in the country who doesn't exist. . . .!*

It was the kind of wild plot that gave us lots of scope, and a great many laughs while writing it. We called it *My Friend Miss Flint*. It had a successful try-out at Windsor, then a tour, and was a hit at the Theatre Royal. Since then it has had a series of increasing productions all over Europe. We did well out of the plays, in particular *Fringe Benefits*, for following its two year run in Paris it was also on French and Swiss television, but I think we both started to realise it was time to again work alone. We were close friends, it had been great fun working together, but Donald had a play he wanted to write, and do what he'd done brilliantly in the past, create a leading role for himself to star in it, while I kept thinking of the burgeoning industry back home. As much as we loved England, the thought of Australia was also seductive. Our son had settled there, and we had a new flat we meant to try out on the next visit.

That plan was a bit premature; we arrived to find the agent had let it for a longer than expected time, so we booked instead to a harbour hotel we'd previously used. Hearing this my father surprised me with a gesture. He had a weekend cottage at Mona Vale that he never used, and now offered it to us for the rest of our visit. In gratitude Marge painted the interior, which had become shabby. He was overcome at her gesture, and I got the feeling no-one had done anything much for him in a long time. He saw little of my brothers and their families. To them, and me, it was perplexing that he still lived in the same dismal house where we'd grown up. None of us liked it: the suburb was an arid place, the house full of cheerless memories. Before we returned to England, Marge and I tried to persuade him to sell it and move to live in Mona Vale. Lakemba was a rambling structure full of bad memories and vacant rooms. Whereas Mona Vale was a charming small cottage with a view of the sea and close to the golf course. Ideal for a man who'd grown up on the beach, and loved swimming and golf. But he'd apparently come to like cats, had started feeding the local strays, and now had a collection he felt unable to abandon. He also had a woman friend with whom he went to the races, but there seemed no-one else in his life. I felt sorry for him, but doubt if he would've appreciated it.

It was during these years that we began to realise the enticing plan to live in both countries had problems. The amount of travel, and being in the right place at the right time could sometimes be difficult. It worked for a while, but in the end started to unsettle us, made us feel like transients; nowhere was truly home, and we finally had to decide where we'd live full time. It wasn't an easy choice; England had been very good to us, and we had many close friends. For twenty years we'd adopted and enjoyed the way of life there, but in the end we decided to settle in Australia. Partly it was because of the government's arts policy. Menzies, in contrast, had always appeared to be indifferent to the arts, and the nineteen-fifties was a sterile era that made many of us seek a life abroad. That Australia had vanished. Books were no longer censored, the arts were flourishing, and it seemed to us this new wave coincided with Gough Whitlam's time in office. This may be giving Gough too much credit, but he was PM when I saw the transformation.

So it was ironic that we expats made our decision to return on the morning of November 11th, 1975— and two hours later heard the shock news that Whitlam had been sacked by the Governor-General he'd appointed. It left us wondering what to do. We had moments of indecision— unlike the confidence years earlier, when people said we were mad to go overseas, and we laughed and took no notice. Maybe that's youthful assurance giving way to middle-age caution— but in the end we felt the decision was the right one. There was a tug of wanting to live again by the beach and hear the sound of the surf; the need to re-acquaint with relatives and friends we'd grown up with, and a slight disenchantment with politics in England.

There was someone else who influenced our choice, and that was Margaret Whitlam. The year Perry was on his visit to see Australia, I was on a fleeting trip to Sydney and found myself invited to Kirribilli House, so I took him with me. It was a party for Margaret, given by people she'd worked with on a television series. I knew some of them, so I caught up with friends, and a short time later saw Perry, sitting and talking to Mrs Whitlam. Just the two of them. Half an hour later they were still busily talking. In fact most of the time, until she was called to give a speech, they sat together conversing, and before we left there he went to shake hands and thank her.

In the taxi afterwards he told me about his evening. She'd noticed his English accent acquired from his years in the UK, and he explained he was trying to decide whether to live here, or remain in England. So she told him about jobs he might find here, and gave him lots of advice.

"When anyone tried to join us, she said she'd see them later. She wanted to know all about us, where we'd lived, where I went to school. She was amazing, so friendly and really interested."

It was no surprise he decided on Australia. If the Prime Minister's wife could devote her evening to helping him, perhaps it was time for us all to come home. It took us another year to rearrange our life, but at the end of 1976 our car was on a ship, our furniture was in a container on another vessel, and we were a Qantas flight to Sydney.

What was really in the back of my mind was an inclination to slow down. We had royalties coming in, particularly from two plays. *Birds on the Wing* and *Fringe Benefits* were both running in Paris, and both would go on earning for a while. I thought I'd write another stage play, then sink into quiet retirement. I was soon to be fifty. Time to play golf, improve my handicap, even catch up on some bridge. But what happened was quite different.

*****

PART SEVEN: RETURNING

The flat at Collaroy was now vacant, and we moved in there to spend our first night at home. For years I'd dreamed of hearing the gentle sound of the surf, the way I remembered it as a boy in my grandmother's beach house, high on the hill in Ramsey Street. But this wasn't high on a hill, this was down on the edge of the sand, and there were no 'gentle sounds' that night–just a fierce wind and a turbulent sea, with waves crashing on the beach. We could hardly hear each other speak, and barely slept. Our much anticipated first night was a comic disaster.

Early next day we had an encounter with the strata management. We went for an early swim, came back and put cossies on the balcony to dry. Soon afterwards came a knock on the door. Two men wearing shorts and long socks arrived to inform us it was against the rules. No laundry to be hung outside. Bathing costumes were considered laundry, they told us, and we were given a list of strata by-laws to study.

"You know what," I said to Marge, when the uninvited had gone, "this place is giving me the shits."

"Me, too," she replied. It was a moment when we might've been tempted to book a return flight to London. But our Kingston house was now let to a tenant, our furniture and the car were somewhere at sea, and before long must be met on arrival.

The following night we had dinner with Googie Withers and John McCallum. We'd met them in London, and spent a week with John in Penang, where his company made a television show, but this was our first visit to their lovely waterfront house at Bayview. We made them laugh about the flat and our encounter with the strata Nazis, and said we'd very likely sell it and look for somewhere else. It brought a moment I've never forgotten.

"We're going to England for six months," Googie said, "Leaving by ship at the weekend. Why not come and live here while we're away."

We could hardly believe it! We tried to discuss rent.

"No rent. Just pay your phone and electricity bills," they told us. "Move in on Sunday. It's yours."

What a perfect way to return to Australia, spending a few months in their elegant house. They were friends, but this was generosity beyond belief. It was an ideal place for entertaining. We caught up with mates we hadn't seen for years, as well as overseas friends who happened to be in Sydney, like actors Trevor Howard and Nigel Havers. Grace Gibson came to visit, remembering a party we'd given her in London. We also rang our daughter Lyn in Canada, and persuaded her to bring Phillip, and spend a few weeks with us. It was part of a devious plan we hoped might persuade her and Rod to consider a move from Vancouver to Sydney.

The house was an eye-opener to her. So was the city. We showed her the highlights, took her to visit friends and relatives who remembered her at the age of five, now a very attractive twenty-six-year-old. My father met her; he even drove all the way to Bayview to visit, and was won over by his granddaughter and first great-grandson. After six weeks we took her to the airport, waved a reluctant farewell, and consoled ourselves that if the plan didn't work, we'd fly via Vancouver each time we went back to London. Then, a few months later, Rod came to visit.

It was one of those winters with blue skies and perfect days. When he said winter in Sydney was warmer than summer in Vancouver, it sounded promising. When he hired a car to drive around appraising areas to live in, it was a hopeful sign. Three months later they phoned from Canada to tell us they were moving to Australia. That was an emotional and wonderful day. I don't remember many better days than that, knowing our family would all be together again in the same country.

During these early months I frequently saw James Gatward, who was producing a TV series here. He and I had often worked together, and we went to lunch at Church Point one day, where he pointed to a craft anchored there. It looked like an old Japanese fishing boat.

"It's called The Krait," he said, and over fish and chips told me how a commando group had sailed it all the way to Singapore, where they blew up Japanese ships in the harbour, and escaped without a single loss. It was one of the amazing exploits of the war.

"What a story!" I said.

"What a film," he replied. "We didn't come here by accident. One of these days I want to produce it, and I want you to write it." Things like that are often said and forgotten, but Jim never forgot. Whenever we met he reminded me it would happen one day. That one day was a long way off, but more about it later.

*****

My first series for the ABC, *Run From the Morning* had been directed by Carl Schultz with a fine cast, led by Michael Aitkins and Barbara Stevens, with Ray Barrett who had just returned from London. It won a TV Times Award for the best script. After this I wrote a film called *Weekemd of Shadow*s, then a TV play called *Money in the Bank*, and not particularly satisfied with either of these, I then wrote a play for myself, called *Once a Tiger*. It was selected by the Actors Forum as a play-reading to raise funds for the North Sydney's Independent Theatre, had a brief run overseas, and since then remains in my desk drawer in the vague hope that someone will like it one day. Time was taken up with a lot of interviews, Bert Newton on television, Philip Adams and many others on radio, and appearances at the Film and Television School.

By the time Googie and John McCallum returned from overseas we had already moved to a house in Collaroy, where I wrote a miniseries for the ABC based on *Golden Soak*, a thriller by Hammond Innes. Filming took place around Broken Hill, and starred Ray Barrett, Elizabeth Alexander, Bill Hunter and Ruth Cracknell. It was well received and led to Innes asking me to adapt another of his books, *Levkas Man*. As it required some research in Greece, one of our favourite places, Marge and I were happy to spend a few weeks in Athens and the Greek islands.

Back in Sydney we began to gradually feel we'd hastily bought the wrong house, and went looking for the right one. Which is how we came to be back in Avalon, startled to find it was transformed from the tiny village we'd known as newly-weds. The same shop on the corner was still there, but now modernised, the same cinema was enlarged, while the streets were crowded with supermarkets and dozens of various stores. We bought a waterfront in secluded Careel Bay, and I discovered the work of Kylie Tennant.

I found a copy of her book *Ride On Stranger* at the local library, started to read it one night, and finished at four in the morning. I asked my then agent, Judy Barry, if she could arrange for me to meet the author.

"Come tomorrow," Kylie invited us, so Judy and I drove up to Blackheath where Kylie and her husband owned an apple orchard. I told her I loved her book, and wanted to take an option in the hope I could persuade the ABC to put it on television. She was pleased at the idea, and agreed to let me have the TV rights. She also insisted we stay for lunch, and afterwards she, Judy and I, went for a walk around her garden that overlooked the Megalong Valley.

"I'm sorry Roddy was so quiet at lunch," she said, referring to her husband who'd been withdrawn, "but we had dreadful news last week. Our son was murdered."

He'd been killed in Sydney, identified under their family name so no newspaper had made the connection with Kylie. Judy and I were shocked that we'd unknowingly intruded at such a time, but Kylie insisted it was what she'd needed. "It was helpful to have something else to think about," she said. "It's good having you here today, and please adapt the book with my blessing."

She was a great lady, and a splendid writer. To me her warm characters leap off the page like those of Dickens, and I class her among the best of our novelists. This feeling was shared by people at the ABC like John Croyston, and with his support it became a miniseries. It was much appreciated when shown, and in following years was repeated several times. It was one of my happiest experiences. At my request it was directed by Carl Schultz, who'd done such a fine job on *Run from The Morning*, the mini-series I'd partly written in England.

Ride on Stranger featured some first rate actors; Noni Hazelhurst, Henri Szeps, Peter Carroll, Michael Aitkens and Margo Lee. In particular it starred Liddy Clark in the key role of Shannon, a rebellious country girl who comes to Sydney in the turbulent 1930s, finding love in commercial radio and being active in radical politics. The character, in part, was based on Kylie's own adventurous youth. We filmed some scenes in the valley below her property, and she came to watch, bringing a load of apples for the cast and crew. I remember she and Liddy meeting, the author with her sun-browned face and silver hair, assessing the actress with her impish smile, and saw Kylie's nod of approval to Carl for the casting.

From the night I read the book it was less than eighteen months before it was screened. This speedy result was aided by John Croyston, who said my enthusiasm to meet Kylie and take a personal option was a vote of confidence. His comments were equally a spur to me; that kind of trust produces loyalty in a writer, and I was fortunate to have a producer and director who didn't want to change a word. It was first shown in 1979, and the script won best adaptation at the 1980 Writers Guild Awards. What a contrast to *The Battlers*, the other Kylie Tennant novel that I adapted, this time for the South Australian Film Corp. It was no fault of either Kylie or me, but it took 15 years until it reached the screen in 1994. Later I'll try to explain what went wrong.

The ABC owned the rights of *The Timeless Land*, a trilogy about a family in early Australia, written by Eleanor Dark. It was a massive project, having once been scheduled to spread over 52 hours, then later scaled down to occupy 26 hours. By the time it was offered to me, the length had been compacted to eight hours!

At first it felt an impossible task—three books, each containing 500 pages, restricted to being told in only eight episodes. I took it on, but it was impossible to cover the entire saga, and I had to leave out sections of this sprawling chronicle. If we'd tried to include everything, it would've been a chaotic failure. In fact it was regarded as a considerable success, and was bought by Paramount for a million dollars, the highest sale until then for any Australian production.

The Timeless Land was made possible by its producer, Ray Alchin, with whom I was to work continuously during the next sixteen years. In the process we became close friends and partners in Resolution Films, a company we later formed to make several of our own shows.

Ray began his career as a film editor, but I met him when he'd just been appointed Head of Production at the ABC studios in French's Forest. He was in his element; the place was a gem, perfect for television. We made many miniseries there, including award winners *1915* and *The Alien Years*, as well as *Sporting Chance*, a series starring Ray Barrett and Liddy Clark.

I'm a keen sports fan, and was very fond of this show with two of my favourite actors. We sometimes ran into trouble with sporting bodies who didn't like critical stories, but you can't have a drama series without conflict. Rugby Union authorities were enraged when I wrote a story of a player who'd been a homosexual, refusing us permission to film on their ovals. They even tried, but failed to persuade league clubs to ban us. Swimming Australia were equally cranky about another script I wrote, where a young girl cracks under the stress of too much training, and the family pressure on her to win an Olympic medal. She starts to shoplift as a protest against the way her life is being manipulated. Both were fiction, set against realistic backgrounds. I enjoyed writing such stories. Others who wrote scripts for this series included Laura Jones. If we occasionally upset the sporting hierarchy, the large audience seemed to prove that viewers liked it.

*****

Around this time I had a call from James Gatward in England. It had been about ten years since our lunch, when he told me about the Krait and the film he intended to make one day. From occasional meetings I knew a lot had happened to him. He'd formed a consortium that won the licence of Southern Television in England, and to his surprise, and mine, was now its CEO. I hadn't seen him for a while when he phoned.

Part Seven: Returning

"Remember the Krait?" he asked.

"I've never forgotten it, Jim," I said, thinking it was just an opening reminder of our past friendship. And the lunch when he told me of the astonishing raid to sink Japanese battleships in Singapore.

"I've got news for you. Our company has done a deal with the Ten network. Do you still want to write it, or are you too busy?"

"You're kidding."

"It's signed and sealed. Do you want to do it?"

"Bloody oath," I said.

"In that case you'll have to fly to London and have a long lunch and probably a dinner with me." I could imagine the grin as he said this. "Would that be a problem?"

"Definitely no problem, Jim."

TV South booked me a hotel suite in Belgravia. They found the batman of Major Lyon, the British officer who'd led the raid, and we spent hours together. The research was invaluable. I flew back to Australia, and wrote a draft script based on the book that told the story of the raid by Ronald McKie. It felt as if filming might start in a month or two; instead, with delays and resignations, another two years passed. Finally I heard the good news that Tony Buckley would be producing. That was when things started to happen.

But there also came unexpected news. Jimmy Gatward was toppled by a palace revolt at his own company, so he was not at the helm, not even there when it was made. Fortunately their head of drama, Graham Benson was just as keen and, with Don Crombie directing, *The Heroes* was a great success. We threw out some ideas of a central love story, and just stuck to basic facts. There was so much drama and tension that it needed no embellishment.

Marge and I flew to London to see it launched, meeting there with Tony Buckley. It was a smash hit—ITV's biggest ever audience, over fifteen million viewers. Tony told us there had apparently been a call from the palace; Her Majesty had requested a private viewing. When I realised the extent of the success, I kept thinking back to the time Jim had told me about the show we'd make one day. My private regret was his absence, as my role in it had derived from our long ago lunch at Church Point.

There had been a second unsuccessful attempt to raid Singapore. We were asked by Graham Benson to work together on this sequel called *Heroes Two: The Return*. I didn't welcome the idea. This was the second part of McKie's book, claiming that after capture the men from the Krait had been regarded by the Japanese as iconic heroes, and were treated with the utmost courteously, then beheaded in the legendary Bushido tradition, after an exchange of salutes with their captors before their deaths.

I felt unable to believe it and did not want to write the screenplay. Even if true, I hated the idea, and felt sure the audience would be sceptical or repelled by these men going so happily to their execution. Two years later we were asked again by TVS. Graham Benson made it clear he particularly wanted the three key Australians; Tony to produce, Donald Crombie to direct, and me to write the script. I still had doubts on its veracity, and luckily discussed it with film producer Lee Robinson.

Lee said he'd once contemplated a similar kind of film, and had been given a box of classified army files. They were in his garage, and because he'd been otherwise involved, had never got around to reading them.

That was when he gave them to me, and they turned out to be vital documents that told a very different story. At the same time it was sheer luck to discover we did not have screen rights to this section of McKie's book. He, like many others, had been misled. The Bushido story had been fabricated to avoid charges of war crimes, and Lee's box of files proved this. It enabled me to write an original screenplay, using the enquiry into what had really happened. Simon Burke played the role of an army investigator who discovers the truth. We had a fortunate escape. If we'd gone ahead two years earlier, we'd have filmed the faked Bushido account; instead it proved to be a far more dramatic true story.

Our only problem was a new script editor at TV South in England. We were continuously harassed by messages from her. Don Crombie and I kept receiving faxes asking for changes to scenes, which had already been filmed the previous day. We had enough trouble caused by torrential rain without this tedious input. In his autobiography Buckley quoted my description of her as 'a true pain in the arse'.

Tony and I go back a long way, long before we actually met—as he was the editor on *Age Of Consent,* and also edited a television series I'd written for Associated Rediffusion in London. It wasn't until I read his book *Behind A Velvet Light Trap* that I realised we'd been linked on these projects for almost forty years, without knowing it.

Marge and I were in Melbourne for the Guild's annual awards night when my father died. We had a call from Lyn with the news, and set out next morning to return to Sydney, but our car broke down at Glenrowan, where Ned Kelly fought his last battle. We had to leave it to be towed to a near garage, took a taxi back to Tullamarine, and caught a plane to Sydney. His death was not a complete surprise, for he'd been in hospital several times in the past year, recently discharging himself by saying he didn't need a hospital to know what was wrong with him.

I was sad that it came at a time when our relationship was so much closer, assisted by Marge and both our children. I felt sorry we were not able to persuade him to move, and he'd spent those solitary years in hislacklustre house. He left it to the friend who went to the races with him, and we assumed it would be sold and become flats. But recently my niece Belinda was driving through Lakemba and took a photo of it to show us. The red brick house on the corner was the same as it looked the day when I left there, seventy years ago. I thought of our unwelcome enclave at the back of the house, and my bedroom, not a proper room at all, just a partition of the area where we had meals. I could not help wondering what kind of house, and what sort of life we would have known, if his wife, our mother, had not died so young.

*****

Touch and Go was a light caper about a female group robbing a bank on Daydream Island, an idea the director Peter Maxwell had in mind. So we went to Queensland and told the manager we'd come to find out the best way to rob his island. We had a cast of fine actresses, Wendy Hughes, Carmen Duncan, Liddy Clark and Barbara Stephens among others. The Queensland Film Corporation helped with the funding, which is how I came to be sitting next to the Premier, Joh Bjelke Petersen and his wife Flo, at the first night in Brisbane. When there was any racy dialogue, Flo speared a reproachful look at Joh, as if he'd risked the reputation of the state by funding this frolic of pretty women getting away with a robbery. Joh, of course, had never seen the script or known its details, but he'd managed to get away with many things himself, during his reign over the Sunshine State. It could've been a better film. David Hannay, one of the producers, was derogatory about the direction, and I had to agree it was lacking in places. Maybe the script was also lacking. The few years that followed, with much better projects for the ABC, was a welcome change.

It was at the Forest Studios, and on location in Western Samoa, that I wrote, and Ray Alchin produced, a mini-series about the turbulent life of Robert Louis Stevenson. It was called *Tusitala*, the name the Samoans gave him, meaning the Teller of Tales. Marge and I went to Western Samoa on a journey to research his life there, being granted the privilege of access to the special Apia library, where a room was insulated against humidity to store all of Stevenson's treasured correspondence. It was a rare and special gesture to be allowed there. The Samoans were wonderfully helpful, very dignified and kind people, though most were desperately poor. Taxis were proof of that; there were rusty holes in the chassis of their cars, and it was slightly alarming to glimpse the road below as we travelled. When most cab drivers were hired by tourists, their first stop was a service station to buy a litre of petrol. A full tank was a luxury not many could afford.

A friendly cab driver took us to the foot of Mount Vaea, the day we climbed it to see Stevenson's grave and the famous inscription on it. The driver asked if he could climb with us. (*Can you imagine a Sydney, London or New York cabbie doing this?*) It was a hot day, a steep climb, and he insisted we pause for an occasional rest. We were glad of his advice; on reaching the summit the pair of us were puffing like steam trains, and the thought crossed my mind about a headline if I corpsed there. The headlines would read: *Writer dies in attempt to view Stevenson's grave*. Imagination is a necessary tool in our work, but there are days when I could do without it!

I embarked on the script of *Tusitala* with enthusiasm, but it did have two unhappy repercussions. Ted Roberts, a friend, had been asked to write it, then fallen out with the producers from Britain's Channel Four who were financing it. As I'd worked with them in the past, they asked me to write it instead. It caused a rift with Ted that never really healed.

There was also a tussle with Don Sharp, who was to direct it. Don had some specific views, and was on the phone from London the moment he heard I was to do the screenplay. He started to tell me how I should tackle it. I had to tell him to shut up and settle down, as I hadn't even signed the contract yet! He wanted to depict Stevenson's early days as a student in France; I felt the sooner he and his wife reached Samoa, the better. We could never agree, but Don as the director prevailed. It was a contrast to other directors with whom I'd enjoyed working, and ended up being shown as a six-hour miniseries. This made the first two hours before he met his wife and scandalised Edinburgh society a bit slow or as one critic declared, rather boring. The blame for this, of course, was levelled at the screenplay.

Later, a producer at Channel Four recut the show, making it four hours, with the opening scene Stevenson and his wife's arrival in Samoa. It was so much better. Channel Four sent me a copy, and I sent it to the ABC Head of Drama in the hope that she might repeat it. She didn't, nor did she even acknowledge its receipt. Despite all this, there were some fine performances. Angela Punch-McGregor was superb as his American wife, while Ray Barrett, playing his best friend, and John Gregg, as the British consul, were both excellent.

This Samoan trip encompassed more time and territory, for it was the start of researching the life of James Cook as well. Marge and I went to Tahiti and the island of Moorea, where Cook's ship had anchored on his last voyage. We had a waterfront bungalow, so each day began with a swim in the water that lapped our doorstep. We spent about eight weeks on this trip, continuing to Rarotonga, an unspoiled gem of a place. There was no work to do there, just a week's R & R in this island paradise with friendly people. It was a truly restful interlude, which was just as well, for the next period from 1982 to 1990 was the busiest of my life.

I adapted Nevil Shute's *The Far Country* for Crawfords, starring Michael York and Sigrid Thornton. It revived memories, for I'd adapted it for radio twenty five years earlier. Also, again for Crawfords, was the first two episodes of *All The Rivers Run*. There were four of us engaged in this, each adapting two episodes; the other writers were Vince Moran, Gwenda Marsh and Colin Free. We spent a pleasant week at Echuca on the Murray River, an ideal spot, for we could see paddle steamers moored outside the room where we had our meetings.

After that were adaptations of *1915*, *The Heroes* and *Naked Under Capricorn*. It was a heavy list of adaptations, followed by original screenplays. *The Lancaster Miller Affair*, *The Heroes Return*, then three mini-series that our company Resolution Films produced: *The Alien Years*, *The Private War of Lucinda Smith*, and our largest production, *Captain James Cook*. A massive amount of work, but it did take eight very busy years.

While all this was going on, a lot was happening on the home front. Our family increased: we now had seven grandchildren swiftly growing up. Marge and I moved house—again! Our defence at this propensity to move so much, was that we both worked at home; we therefore lived in a house 24/7 which, in my wife's accepted wisdom, was twice as long than most people! We enjoyed Careel Bay, but at times it felt remote, there was a lot of travel up and down, so we found a perfect house in Cremorne, until tempted a few years later, by one even more perfect, on the slopes of Balmoral.

This had a magnificent view from the study, across the harbour to North and South Head. It was so magnetic that before long I had to move to a back room, where the only view was a blank wall, and attention would not be diverted by Manly ferries, or occasional liners heading out to the rest of the world.

In between times we acquired an ancient weekender on the Wyong River which we restored. It was a rare old farmhouse, one of the first homes in the district. The restoration began with a new roof. Then we stripped the fibro walls, replaced them with weatherboard, and built a veranda. It was great therapy after writing all week, to go there and do some manual work. The grandchildren loved the place as well. There were trees to climb, a large garden for games, and the wide river to swim in. We bought canoes for them, and for over five years enjoyed an idyllic life between the elegance of Balmoral and tranquil weekends on the river.

It was during this period that Kylie Tennant was ill with cancer, and the South Australian Film Corporation had at last agreed to film her book *The Battlers*. It had been sitting with them for what seemed like half a lifetime, as they'd expressed interest but then did little about it. I kept hoping because I wanted the miniseries made while Kylie was alive, as she'd insisted for years that no-one else could have the screen rights. These extended delays had begun to make my hope almost impossible. When she was taken to hospital we had a pact, so at least she could know it would be made. I'd visit her again and we'd sign the contract together, but there was yet another unnecessary legal delay over that, and she died before it could happen. It was to be three more frustrating years before filming began, making a total of fourteen years since *Ride On Stranger*.

It should have better; *Battlers* was a stronger story, people trying to survive in the depths of the great depression. One of Kylie's gifts was the rich characters she interwove in the manner of classic novels. This was marvellous in a book, but sometimes imposed problems for adaptation. I had no interference at the ABC, and was able to avoid some of her fascinating detours. Kylie had no argument with that.

"The book is my work, the television's yours," she said, with her usual generosity, but we were dealing with different people this time.

Both the story editor and producer wanted to add extra incidents to my early drafts, on the basis that these were "too good to leave out." While in part agreeing, I did point out the script was growing, and not everything could be included. We were continually making additions. *"Too good to leave out"* became a phrase that worried me. By the third draft the script was vastly over length, and still growing. A lot of people in Adelaide seemed to have this urge to add scenes, and nobody wanted anything deleted. Timings were made, after which I was told my fears were quite ridiculous, the script was definitely not long. Another expert timer declared that far from being long, it was actually too short, and needed extra scenes.

From experience I felt this was impossible, but no-one, including the well-known and experienced director, would listen. Once the filming began, there seemed to be little communication; they were in Adelaide, I was in Yarramalong, not aware of progress or growing trouble. But soon it became apparent we were vastly over length. When it was too late there was no longer a dispute; without major surgery it would not only be much too long, but the budget would run out of money.

Dismay and panic were now apparent in South Australia. Scenes had to be cut, but they could only be deleted from the final hour, because it had been filmed in sequence. Frantic cuts had already been made, some I knew nothing about, until receiving the news of them by fax in Sydney. It was chaotic. A complete rewrite of the final hour was necessary, and I was asked to cut it to ribbons. How on earth could their 'expert timer', the one who insisted it was too short, have been so totally wrong? Why didn't the director, or anyone else involved, realise the disaster before it was almost too late?

Although it was ruthlessly cut and patched together, I felt the result was disastrous. It was an example of what can happen when there is no communication between the director and writer. The director of *The Battlers* made no contact during the wreckage, when the final sixty minutes had to be slashed, almost in half. Nor did I ever hear from him again. What a difference to the way we worked in *Ride On Stranger*, a production where we were all on the same side.

*****

PART EIGHT: COOK AND THE ABC

Our company Resolution Films was created to make a mini-series about Captain James Cook, intending to call it *The Wind and The Stars*. I'd been asked to write it by the ABC several years earlier, and they had big plans for it. But then came sudden changes at the corporation, with a new head of television, Richard Thomas, who no longer wanted period drama. So my project on Cook was dropped which I regretted, as I'd done a lot of research, and felt these, ending up in a bottom drawer, were some of the best scripts I'd written.

The research had made me realise Cook had been a victim of the British class system, and, having seen this at close quarters when we lived there, it made the character far more interesting. No longer merely an historical figure, he had problems and ambitions, and came alive. We think of him as **Captain** Cook, a naval deity, but he was not even a lieutenant when the first voyage was planned. He was selected by the affluent Joseph Banks, who wanted a sailor to navigate the ship, allowing Banks to rule his large entourage of scientists and botanists who filled the main cabin. When they returned after the first great voyage across the world, it was Banks lionised in the streets of London, as he drove to the palace in a gilded carriage. It was Banks chosen to be congratulated and knighted by the King, while Cook went home to his wife and children in their modest East End cottage.

It was the characters of James Cook and his wife who attracted me. They must have resented the impression he had merely steered the ship for his social superiors. Cook surely felt upset, having to wait for the admiralty's judgement on whether the journey had been worthwhile, and would he receive promotion, or be ignored? After all, it was well known that his first youthful job had been serving in a shop. And how would his wife react to this treatment of her husband after his epic three year voyage, during which she had born one child, but lost another through illness?

In hindsight I was fortunate the ABC was no longer interested, as I was able to regain copyright of the scripts and decided to rewrite them. By forming the Resolution Films company with Ray Alchin and Geoff Daniels we became our own masters, and could ignore the budget constraints that previously dictated it could only be six hours in length.

I always felt that was too brief, and expanded it to eight hours. Then we set out to raise the estimated cost of ten million dollars, or the scripts would go back into a drawer, this time to surely stay there.

Ten million was a big budget for Australian television in the 1980's, but there was no way it could be less. Period drama is always expensive. This contained not only a long list of scenes to be filmed at sea, as well as part of the story requiring Pacific islands with their native inhabitants needed for crowd scenes. That was just the start; there were London dockyards, New Zealand and Australian sites, the three different journeys and their crews, plus a large cast and locations that looked like parts of eighteenth-century England.

Hearing this, I began to feel writing the script had been the easiest part of the venture.

Geoff started to make the rounds of investment banks and brokers, trying to interest them. Meanwhile Revcom, a French company run by Michel Noll in Paris, showed interest. They gave us $20,000 towards expenses, as a loan to be repaid if they didn't participate. We used it to fund a visit to Auckland, where the head of NZ TV read the scripts and liked them enough to say they'd be willing to invest two million dollars in the production.

Wow! We were up and away, I thought.

Marge and I went overseas to meet with Michel Noll. He'd just bought a house in the south of France, so we ended up among the cavorting rich at Cap d'Antibes while I told him about New Zealand and their two million. Michel got highly excited and spent the rest of the day doing sums on notepaper.

"I think I can raise the rest," he said, so we cautiously celebrated that night. He left the next day for Paris, to do more calculations. We went to spend a few days with friends in Montreal, before a meeting in New York with Dino di Laurentis who'd made the film *Mutiny On The Bounty* and owned the ship featured in it. There was a chance we could rent the 'Bounty', as it was known. If so we were truly on our way; it had been quicker and easier than we'd imagined. A few days and we'd be casting, looking for an actor to play Cook. My own first thought was Nigel Havers.

Marge and I had the pleasure of driving through the Adirondacks that autumn with our Canadian friends, but New York became our first setback. Dino was no longer interested. One of his acolytes met me to explain the 'Bounty' was now for sale, and no longer for hire.

From the bad news we flew back to Auckland, so I could meet again with the head of New Zealand television. The news there was even worse. Local producers had become furious on hearing two million of their dollars would be used to fund an Aussie production. Australia was not a favorite neighbour ever since the under-arm bowling incident. The board of NZ TV had listened to the uproar and surrendered. There were sincere regrets, but the two million was no longer available.

Michel, by now expecting good news in Paris, was dismayed by this financial setback. He had been counting on the NZ investment. For some time it seemed like a dead end, we didn't have a boat, or any money. Fortunately we kept quiet about these double disasters. It was not any cleverness on our part, we were simply stunned by the way we'd hit a brick wall, and not anxious to advertise it.

About this time I went to a 'wrap' party at the Forest Studios, to celebrate the end of filming the *1915* series. I was approached there by an ABC executive, Diana Quinter. She hadn't come to congratulate; this was an angry woman with a private protest. She wanted to know why we had chosen to deal with New Zealand Broadcasting. Fortunately she hadn't heard of our setbacks, and she didn't give me a chance to explain it.

"Why not the ABC?" she demanded, and before I could answer she hit me with another salvo. "What's wrong with us?" she asked.

"You don't want the show. You don't like it," I said.

"Who the hell told you that?"

"Richard Thomas."

"Well, he's gone," Di replied.

"He might've gone, but his philosophy lingers on," I answered.

"This is ridiculous," she said. "A lot of us want it. We're really pissed off. After all the shows you've written for us, you won't even talk to us. We should be in on this. It's a perfect vehicle for the ABC."

I could see she was serious, and Di was a lady who wielded a lot of power in the corporation corridors. So I pointed across at the bulky figure of Geoff Daniels whom she knew from years of working with him.

"I'm just the scribe," I said. "Go and talk to him. You can say I think we should be making it right here, in the Forest Studios."

I watched her make her way through the crowded party, taking Geoff by the arm, and steering him aside for a chat.

Within days we had an agreement with the ABC. They would supply crew and studios, in return for Australian TV rights. Now it was up to Noll, but a lot of people kept expressing doubts he could raise the rest. Rumours started circulating that he wasn't reliable. Michel rang me late at night and insisted he had seven million.

"It was eight, Michel," I reminded him. "Reduced to eight million now the ABC is in for a share of the costs."

"Well, eight if necessary," he said, sounding reluctant.

That was how it stayed for the next few days; Geoff kept talking to the local money moguls on the basis we could make it under the tax advantaged 10BA scheme, while Michel kept ringing to insist that he could finance it.

Meanwhile the boat we wanted so badly, the 'Bounty' had been virtually sold to an Australian Adventure group. They asked for an urgent meeting with us, where we were told they wanted to buy the boat, but needed help. We could have the 'Bounty' delivered to us in Tahiti, fully crewed for the filming on Moorea, then brought to Sydney by its crew to complete the filming here. It was ours for four months, or more if we needed it, at a single upfront fee of one million dollars. If we paid them that, they could buy the boat.

A million bucks! At first hearing it sounded like a killer, because we had almost nothing in the bank. But on reflection it was not a bad deal. In fact, it began to feel like a very good one. The 'Bounty' was a perfect vessel, the ship we'd always wanted. We couldn't get a better one, and this contract would cover all crew costs, the months of sailing, and would be ideal for nautical scenes that would otherwise need sets being built in the studio. So we said yes, trying to look as if we had the money in the bank. It was nerve-racking after they'd gone and we were alone in my living room, where the meeting took place.

"It's up to Michel," Geoff said, "he has to pee or get off the pot." We all knew it. If he didn't agree, we could be in serious *merde*.

Geoff rang him that night. Michel Noll provided the needed million dollars for the boat, and said the rest of the money would be paid, but there was a condition. It proved to be more than a condition, it felt like an ultimate deal breaker, an absolute and certain killer. He wanted eight overseas actors to be cast in the show. We said it was impossible. He refused to budge, saying he must have eight, or else it was goodbye. It felt like winning a lottery, to find out we'd just lost the ticket.

Actors Equity had strict guidelines on imports. Too often in the past films had been made here with overseas stars, and Aussie actors had to play supporting roles. These days Equity made the rules, allowing one actor, rarely ever two, and never EIGHT. From my own experience I felt sure it would be hopeless. Sometimes they'd even reject just one. The star of *Chariots Of Fire*, Ian Charleson, had liked my script of *The Lancaster Miller Affair*, and wanted to play the lead, but Equity refused to allow it. How would they agree to eight foreign actors, when they wouldn't allow an Oscar nominee like Charleson? Michel insisted on the imports, otherwise there was no way he could raise seven million. *Eight million*, I kept reminding him. He kept reminding me he needed actors from countries where he had access to finance: France, Germany and Spain. The arithmetic made sense, but the request felt impossible. We needed a miracle. Ray Alchin had always been on good terms with Equity, so we nominated him to take on the herculean task.

"Thanks a heap," he said.

I still don't know how Ray managed it—but he achieved the impossible miracle. Equity agreed!! We could bring in eight actors, but only on one condition. James Cook must be played by an Australian. But .....who? We passed on Bryan Brown. Bud Tingwell was too old. English Nigel Havers, was out. Sam Neill (a token Aussie) was working. So was John Waters. We were actually in Moorea searching for locations, when a name was faxed from the ABC's casting director, Jennifer Allen. *What about Keith Michel*, she wrote.

Why not, I thought, remembering his electric performance as Henry the Eighth. So what if he was older than Cook? Keith kept himself fit and didn't look his age. Equity accepted Keith. So did Noll. I thought Jennifer Allen was an absolute genius. A last we were in business, four years after writing the revived scripts. In the meantime I'd written other screenplays, while this had been on the back burner, with us doubting it would ever happen. But at last it did; we had the finance, the boat, and now we had the right star. We also had a director. Laurence Gordon-Clark was English. When the first scenes were shot on Moorea, I was in Sydney awaiting the rushes. The moment I saw them I felt a thrill. There was real excitement on the screen. After the years of waiting, all the frequent trips, the near misses, the stress, at last all that effort was going to be worthwhile.

And it was. I still treasure the reviews. *$10 Million mini-series on Captain Cook is flawless* was a headline, and there were plaudits in the press from Anna Murdock and others. My only disappointment, a massive one, was the title. Michel Noll began to call it *Captain James Cook*, saying my title did not translate. Of course it did. A German author wrote a book from my scripts calling it *Wind und Sterne*. I expressed my concern to the ABC, who faithfully promised they'd keep my original title. This pledge was made at a festive gala, a full house where their top brass spouted generous praise about my four-year battle to get it made. But in the end, after all their flowery words the promise was a lie. I remember David Williamson telling me how much he liked the show, but asked why I'd dropped a great title like *The Wind and the Stars* for such a bloody awful one?

At least it won the viewers. It was scheduled over a week—two hours on successive week nights at 8.30, then the last two hours on the prime Sunday night spot. The commercial channels threw their best films against it, but it won all the ratings each time, including the Sunday night. When it was over I had calls from many friends, in particular from ninety-year-old friend, film director Ken Hall. That was a tribute I welcomed.

During the long months it took to film Cook, I wrote my tenth and last mini-series for the ABC. It was something that had been discussed a few years earlier, under the working title of SAGA, because nobody could decide what it was going to be. To explain this, I'd been asked to write a special television series that would be a historical drama shown at the time of the forthcoming bi-centenary. The concept went out the window during the Thomas era, so I had put all the research notes aside.

But among those notes was the germ of an idea that I'd always wanted to write as a novel, so I made time to start work on it. The idea began to grow and excite me, which meant no day passed without adding more pages, until there was what felt like the chapters of a growing novel. I did a word count, and found I'd written 30,000 words in what seemed like just a few weeks.

As a story it began in Broken Hill where a man makes a shady fortune, escapes arrest and becomes rich. He returns to his wife and daughter in Sydney, buying his way into politics at a time when the New South Wales parliament was at its most corrupt. His daughter Elizabeth, aged seventeen, meets and falls in love with a young German immigrant. They run away to start a new life in South Australia. The story is balanced between her father's political career in Sydney, and his daughter's life in the Barossa Valley when the 1914 war breaks out.

It led to a shameful period in Australian history that has always intrigued me, the treatment of Germans in our country during the First World War. These were people who had migrated here, fleeing from tyranny in their own land. They raised families, started vineyards and were assimilated into Australian life. Yet suddenly they were the enemy, accused of being spies and interned in the spurious name of patriotism. I was deeply involved with it, and the word count had reached 40,000, when the ABC remembered they'd asked me to write a 'saga' for the bicentenary. So where was it? Had I done it? Well, no, not after the brush-off by Thomas. But he'd gone, and it was Ray Alchin, my close friend, who'd be blamed if I admitted I'd actually entirely forgotten the Saga!

I really didn't want to stop writing it as a novel. I had a feeling I was on to something that had not been tackled, but because our company would produce it, and Ray had depended on this, I changed course. The 40,000 words went into a bottom drawer, and became a TV miniseries instead. My title was *A Hill of Roses*, because the authorities seized on the name Barossa, saying it was Germanic and must be changed. Just in time they found it was Spanish and meant a hill of roses.

Too soft for a title declared Sandra Levy, now the drama Czarina at the ABC. She didn't enthuse about the show either, not her kind of thing she told me candidly, but she had a few valid suggestions, and after tossing around titles we settled on *The Alien Years*. Filming was at Hahndorf and Bethany in the Barossa Valley. It was there we needed a broken down vineyard. Ray had a theory the place to find locations was at a local pub. So we had a couple of beers and asked if anyone knew of a decrepit vineyard where we could film. Sure enough someone did. It was just five minutes from town, and perfect for what we had in mind.

Unlike Cook this show only had modest publicity, so we were surprised by its impact. The comments about it lasted for months on a program called *Back Chat*, where the audience aired their views. Some were upset, asking why I wanted to write such a distressing story of Australian behaviour on our birthday year; others said since we were 200 years old, it was time we learned things that had been hidden from the history books. I found this mixed response immensely satisfying. Mrs Lehmann, of the wine-making family, declared the show was a healing process.

In 1989 the script won the Australian Writers Guild award for the best original screenplay. Sandra Levy, while still maintaining it was not to her taste, did ask if I wanted to do a sequel. I thanked her, but rejected the offer, partly because I felt it might be more satisfying one day to return to the incomplete novel. About six years later, after we'd moved to the Central Coast and entirely due to my wife, I did exactly that.

*****

PART NINE: WHAT'S A COMPUTER?

When I first wrote short stories it was with a pen. Then I saved to buy a typewriter, but never learned to type properly. Even when I made the quantum leap to an electric portable, I was still a two-finger typist. When the rest of the world moved to computers, I remained the last of the Luddites. Then came the day we closed the Resolution Film office, and Geoff Daniels gave the Apple machine to Marge, knowing she could use a computer. I looked at it a few times then, still using two fingers, tried to see how it felt by typing a make-believe dialogue between us.

Me: How's this thing supposed to work?

Marge: Just tap the keys. Have another go. It won't bite you.

Me: Are you sure? Why does everyone like them?

Marge: They save paper. You delete mistakes, not tear up pages.

Me: Is this going to be a paperless world?

Marge: That's the objective.

Me: Bugger!!!! Why did everything just disappear?

Marge: Because you pressed the wrong button.

So I got trapped into Apple, then Microsoft, and gradually a brand new method of writing. I learned not to press the wrong button, but nothing else changed. My two fingers still tap the keyboard, and the paperless world was a joke. I now revise, then reprint, using more paper than ever.

Along with this new way to write, we also changed location again. Balmoral was enjoyable with its fine view, but in summer it was a tourist magnet, and our street resembled a parking lot. We'd had over five years of it, and liked the idea of a change, particularly when we saw a ten-acre property for sale on the fringe of the Yarramalong Valley.

Another reason prompted this; I was becoming tired of television. It was little wonder. In the sixteen years since coming home, I'd written eighteen mini-series, a stage play, and three films. I wanted a break, then something different, which meant trying to write novels. Unsure where this would lead, we both felt a quieter country life might be the prudent answer. So in 1991 we bought the house with ten acres, about an hour's drive from Sydney. In some ways the acreage and state forest behind it to create privacy was like Ashtead. The rambling house had several extra bedrooms for when grandchildren wanted to stay, it had a perfect study with no distracting view, and a massive room upstairs that Marge converted into her studio.

It was after this move that I made contact with Meg Labrum of the National Film and Sound Archive in Canberra. The task of finding storage for scripts and papers as we moved house, led to a flow of letters with Meg, and a lasting friendship as she arranged donations of my work from the past fifty years. These extracts are from our letters in 1991.

Dear Peter
Your collection sounds wonderful, but at present is unlisted. I received a rough idea of it from the Rick Raftos Agency, but a detailed list would be an enormous help, as well as assisting with

valuations should you proceed with your donation. An estimate of the physical size and idea of boxes required, would greatly assist. Is such a listing possible? On the question of the taxation incentives for the Arts Scheme, the National Archive is happy to discuss details of how donation can be made, but it is important to note that in our current situation, if we accepted your deposit access, could not be provided before late 1993. May I ask you for any conditions attached to this material, and I will follow with a formal response. Looking forward to your reply. Regards, Meg.

Dear Meg, 20/1/1992
First, a Happy New Year, and thank you for interest in the collection. My preference would be for it to go to the Film and Sound Archive, for students and writers to have access. In a way it might be a record of many years as a writer, when people said: "Yes, but what do you do for a living", through tough days in radio, then better times overseas. Since 1976 when I came home there have been 15 produced miniseries. There is also documentation of unproduced work, with correspondence attached. I have just two small problems at the moment. Problem One: I have just moved house, and would really like to dispose of all these boxes. It seems you may not be able to receive them before late 1993, which sounds close to 1994, and therefore two years away. Problem two. The tax incentive. I'm told it limits tax relief to the year of donation. In our industry there is no way of telling what the next year, or even the present one, might be worth. At the moment I'm trying to write a novel, so this year will produce almost no income. If the novel is published and sells as a movie, next year might be a bonanza. But if the book is a fizzer ... no bonanza, therefore no point in a tax deduction if I don't owe tax. I hope you see what I mean. Forward planning is almost impossible, but the tax incentive for the arts scheme seems to require both a crystal ball and forward planning. With best wishes, Sincerely, Peter.

Dear Meg,
Here is a follow up to my previous fax, with 8 pages listing all the documents and other items. To give you an idea of the physical volume I think a lot of storage boxes, possibly fifty may be necessary. My press clippings are optional: if not of interest, my kids might like to use them for target practice on their dartboard.

Dear Peter,
Many thanks for your unexpected and detailed description of the Yeldham papers! We agree fifty boxes will be necessary. It has made everything clear, and the Archive would love to include this material in the national collection. We will need to chat about practical things like packing and pickups, and whether there is any part of this collection which you wish restricted. My thanks for such a big effort to get the ball rolling. With Best Wishes, Meg.

The first donation was by far the largest, covering the work done in England as well as all the miniseries since coming home. I made two smaller contributions after this, one containing some disappointments like *The Battlers*, and a few that were never made including an attempt to tell the story of Darcy Dugan.

Meg and I remained in touch. In 2006 there was a letter from her, proposing a special Q @ A session at the Archive theatre in Canberra, inviting me to appear with her on stage. It was a memorable occasion, with a full house of film buffs and students. She kept them entertained by questions for me to answer, even getting me to reveal how Terry Nation found a name for his invention, the Daleks. Her idea was a great success. I think we enjoyed it as much as the audience did.

Returning to the new life spent in the Yarramalong Valley, a place we grew to love, I started to write my first novel, a thriller called *Reprisal*. It was about three conscripts sent to Vietnam, who return to their country that jeers and abuses them for taking part in the war. Shocked and angered by this, they successfully rob a bank and retire into wealthy obscurity, until the past starts to catch up with them.

Ted Willis, on a visit from England, came to spend the weekend with us. "You promised to write a novel since we met, 20 years ago" he said, which seemed like my cue to display the almost finished manuscript, and promising I'd send him a copy if it ever found a published. To our sorrow Ted died of a heart attack a few months before that happened. He was one of our early close British friends, and had dedicated a book to us, as I did to his memory, when *Reprisal* was published. Before this, I started work on a second book in case too many rejections sapped my confidence. It was just as well, because there were numerous rebuffs on *Reprisal*. Pan Macmillan liked it, but told my agent they would wait to see another book, if I got around to writing one. I'd actually finished this second book when *Reprisal* was accepted by a small and almost unknown Sydney firm in 1994. It was a thrill to pass a bookshop and see it in print. I could only wish there'd been more bookshops. However friends made purchases, and seemed to like it. So, I'm glad to say, did the critics. Both *The Herald*, and Graeme Blundell in *The Australian*, listed it among the best thrillers of the year. Because of this, *Reprisal* had an extra lease of life, bought by Readers Digest Books, and published overseas in a volume along with eminent names—Fredrick Forsythe, Dick Francis and Robert Harris. A few years later it became a telemovie for Channel Nine.

Meanwhile my agent sent the second book to Pan Macmillan, and Cate Paterson promptly accepted it. This was another thriller, called *Without Warning*, and it also received good crits. It was nominated for a Ned Kelly award, and became another telemovie for the Nine Network. The Network's original idea had been a TV series to feature the main characters in *Reprisal*. I was not certain of this; it seemed like a path back to television, stuck with a weekly stream of episodes, but the arrival of the second book changed things. Channel Nine decided both novels should become telemovies. By this time Ray Alchin had joined James Davern at his company JNP, and they did a deal with the Nine network to produce them. Then I was asked to write a script that could be third film, making it a prestige package of three films on successive films under my name.

Unexpectedly, filming *Reprisal* turned out to be a very difficult task, and a somewhat hellish experience for all concerned, especially Jim, Ray and me. On day one, with actors on the set and the camera focused, the television executives became nervous about the concept they'd bought with such enthusiasm. They suddenly found it a problem to accept my disillusioned Vets could not only rob a bank, but then settle down in a placid seaside town where they became upright citizens.

"These men are crooks, so they can't live happily ever after," was the protest from Nine's Head of Drama. He seemed to have forgotten it was the story they'd bought, and his next suggestion proved it. "Couldn't it be for charity? Let them do it as a fund-raising for a children's hospital?'

"For God's sake, be real," I think I almost shouted. "They were conscripted, then came home to be met by abuse. Everyone seemed to forget the bloody government had forced them to go there. They were treated like shit." As for his notion of them robbing banks for charity, I tried to point out it was an out-of-date American idea, belonging back in the days of black and white television. I suggested rather than make ourselves look idiotic, let's not make the film at all. Which was bluff, and far too late; I'd sold the rights, but it did shut them up about the antiquated idea of these former soldiers robbing a bank for charity.

The experience of turning these books into screenplays taught me the most difficult adaptation was converting one's novels into a film. I adapted many books into movies; *Age of Consent*, *The Liquidator* and *Comedy Man* among them, while for TV there was *The Timeless Land*, *Far Country* and others. They all had their problems. Books don't always transfer easily to the screen. There is often more content in a novel, which can mean scenes may need to be omitted, and characters deleted. Adapting is, on these occasions, the art of being ruthless. But if this means being ruthless with one's own novel, what then? Sometimes these scenes contain the most interesting characters. They're the ones that made writing the novel a pleasure, but if they don't assist the screenplay, then they have to go! It becomes an exercise in self-flagellation.

In adapting *Reprisal* the major loss was deleting the friendship that grew between the main robber and the detective sent to trace and arrest him. The network declared it slowed the story. Yet it was a vital element of the novel. Everyone who read the book said this was the best part. Another problem was the flashbacks to the actual robbery. A key factor in the book was one of the wives being pregnant, giving birth the night of the robbery to twins forcing a delay. The row, with the husband refusing to rob a bank the night his wife was in labour gave the book a lot of drama, but this and much of the robbery was dropped. Having sold the rights to the network, its minions had the upper hand, but I regretted losing these details. Like Jim and Ray, I was never really happy with the finished product, after the loss of those sub-plots.

It had been so easy as a book. I wrote it to please myself, and had just two brief meetings with the editor, who made a couple of minor suggestions. She said I was free to ignore these, because it was my work if I disagreed with her suggestions. This attitude was so different to dictates in movies and television, both often made by committees these days. It was what had turned me off TV. You have to please far too many people, and the result can only be a compromise.

A final blow; the promised three film package never happened. Each film was shown far apart, not linked as written and signed in my contract.

*****

I went from arguments with Channel Nine, back to more peaceful days of writing books. By now I was engaged in a third thriller called *Two Sides of a Triangle*, set mostly in South East Asia. Because of this, Pan Macmillan had me cast as a thriller writer. Unknowingly, I was about to toss a spanner in the works and make things less peaceful. It began one day when I found Marge reading the Barossa manuscript, the 40,000 words in the bottom drawer that had become *The Alien Years* on the ABC.

"What a waste," she said.

"You really think so?"

"Truly. Do me a favour. Read it again, and see what you think."

So I re-read it the next day, and agreed with her. I'd been rash to sacrifice it on television, now past its viewing and forgotten. I did think that chunk of words would be an easy start, resuming on page 40,001, but then decided against this. With that resolved I began a rewrite from page one.

For months I worked on the Barossa story in tandem with *Two Sides of a Triangle*. It is something I'd never done before, and am unlikely to try again, but I wanted to commit to this new book despite my contract to complete the thriller. Cate Paterson was waiting for its arrival, but not expecting anything else. She had no idea of the Barossa story, now called *A Bitter Harvest*, where all the characters were coming alive, and new ones were evolving with each chapter.

I had to stop it and finish *Two Sides*, which I did and sent it to Cate. She told me she liked it, an editor was assigned, and after that I was able to concentrate entirely on World War One and the turmoil in the Barossa. There were long days and late nights, but I found I was hardly ever tired. When writing feels good, it may be a delusion, but I don't notice fatigue. I was aware of making some major changes, as the book became quite unlike the television script of *The Alien Years*.

Different things happened, new people emerged. The politician and his daughter remained central, but his grandson was a new addition, a major and important character. It was, of fifteen novels, the one I most enjoyed writing. The story had become so real. In September I sent it to Pan Macmillan, and waited for a reply. When it came at first I thought it was a joke. They were not sure if they even wanted to read it!!

But no-one was joking, I finally realised, and their reaction left me shell-shocked. I asked why, and was told they had always classified me as a thriller writer and expected a regular output of crime stories. It was pointed out I'd already written three of them; they had published *Without Warning*, pleased it had been a runner up in the Ned Kelly awards, and were about to publish my new thriller. By now I realised nobody was happy about the arrival of this new surprise. I'd upset the apple cart, but it had never occurred to me that new writers were labelled by their first novels. Crime was the slot they'd assumed I'd occupy, not fooling around writing something so completely different.

I finally had to ask if anyone was going to bother reading it, or should I ask my agent to try another publisher. After days of stress and phone calls there came a reluctant agreement, the manuscript would be given to selected readers for an assessment. I had to wait in anxiety until the comments arrived.

To my relief they were positive, even enthusiastic. Cate phoned to pass on the news, and said it would be published in the new year after a reasonable gap to allow readers to digest *Two Sides of a Triangle*, which she assumed would be my last thriller. By that comment I could see how I'd crossed lines and caused a minor chaos. Madonna Duffy was chosen as editor, and it was pulished in 1997. Soon afterwards Pan Macmillan did a second print, and twelve years later it was republished by Penguin I feel it was my best novel. It received plaudits from many unexpected quarters: *An epic read, totally absorbing* said the Herald. *A fascinating journey into the past,* came from the *Brisbane News*. *The Master of the Australian historical blockbuster* was a critic's tag too exciting to ignore, and after that was spread on the cover of other future books. Being categorized as a crime writer was over. I'd enjoyed writing *A Bitter Harvest* so much the future had to be novels from our extensive history.

The next book, *The Currency Lads* was set in early Sydney just after it was gazetted as a city. In 1840 homes were being built and gas lighting was installed in the streets. Australia was attracting immigrants to join the growing population of the native born, when Britain chose to resume the transport of convicts. It was a rash and arrogant decision that caused disbelief at first, then rising anger and threats of civil war and calls for independence.

The first characters I had in mind were two boys, the sons of convicts, who grow up amid these years, both proud of their status of being native born. Both became adults by the time of the arrival of the convict ship, and play vital roles in the turmoil. One of them, Mathew Conway, is the son of a printer and grows up assisting his father until he becomes a journalist. The other, Daniel Johnson, is an orphan adopted by the Conway family, and earns a living rowing people across the harbour, and by the age of twenty he owns an ocean-going schooner. His life is transformed when he meets an artist in the colony, a free settler earning her living as a governess. I wrote a brief scene of her meeting Daniel when she is sketching his ship from the Botanic Gardens. That was all I intended, but she developed on the page and in my mind by falling in love with him, becoming a major figure in the story. It was the way a sudden new character can surface like this and almost take over. I love the surprise when it happens like this, giving the story, and even the writer, an unexpected change of direction.

It was the second book of mine bought by Readers Digest for its series of *Select Editions*, and published around the world in company with Robert Harris and other authors It was also translated and published in Italy, and would almost certainly have become a film, but for an unexpected and tragic event.

A few weeks after publication Ray Alchin read it and rang me in high excitement. He wanted it for a film, and already had plans worked out. We would shoot all the sequences of period Sydney the way we had with the Captain Cook scenes; it meant filming with today's high buildings in the background, then use the same device to turn the modern skyscrapers into an 18th century background. All other scenes of Sydney Town in the period would be no problem, he reminded me. We had done it before, when we made *The Timeless Land*.

His enthusiasm thrilled me. We agreed to meet after the weekend to plan it. The next day, Saturday, Marge and I had been to dinner with friends. We came home to a message from his wife. Appalling, unbelievable news. He had played tennis that afternoon, collapsing on the court with a heart attack, and dying in hospital.

It wasn't just the loss of a very close friend. Many people in the industry felt bereft. Ray was the energy, the enthusiasm, first at the ABC, later as head of Revcom in Sydney, then at JNP with Jim Davern. Wherever he went he generated a passion for making movies. Films for the big or small screen were his life since his early days as an editor. I missed that vitality. We'd worked together for many years, and he'd produced most of what I'd written for the ABC, as well as the entire output of our own company. We shared so many plans for the future. There are some in your life who are irreplaceable, and for me Ray Alchin was one of them. I spoke at his funeral, and wrote his obituary for *The Herald* and *The Australian* newspapers.

Part Nine: What's a Computer?

It had been a long time since meeting with Michael Craig, who starred in *The Timeless Land* and later directed a reading of my stage play *Once A Tiger*. He was now one of the main doctors in a long running ABC series *GP*. "They'd love you to write a script for them," he said, when we met at a party for Ray Barrett's birthday.

I was not so sure. Although I'd written a lot of the ABC's television in a past decade, the power brokers had changed, and I was no longer on their A list. Mike insisted they'd be keen, declaring it was easy. Having written several episodes himself, I thought he should know, and found myself talked into it. The following day producer Carol Williams rang to propose I write a special two-hour movie version. It was a surprise, and a challenge to write a film version. In my early London days when on various TV series, we'd arrive with a story idea, then go off and write it. Often this was considered the final draft, and we then attended the reading. But at the ABC I soon found out it would not be like that. Not at all like it. Writing *GP* was a strict formula, with the guidelines set in concrete.

Our first day should have been a warning. It was a meeting of a great many people packed into a small room, presided over by the producer, and attended by a plethora of story editors. Not only the editor of the forthcoming film, but editors of past episodes as well as future ones. In addition there was a set designer, an associate producer, a production manager, a researcher and a medical adviser. There were others, whose reason for being there escaped me, but it seemed as if more people were needed for this than any of the feature films I'd written. An assistant hung up a large board on which was listed THE MOVIE: Episodes 164-165. I arrived with a few ideas, to find there was already a storyline decided for me. One of the doctors would fall in love with a Chinese-Australian girl.

During that first day I learned the schedule. There'd be another meeting like this in a week's time, then my full scene breakdown must be ready two weeks later, followed by four weeks in which I had to write the first draft. This would be followed by another meeting, with notes on the draft, then the second draft, after which there would be a meeting with the director, followed by the third draft. By then I was aware I'd landed myself into a total nightmare.

After just one day I felt as if we were discussing a final screenplay, but I hadn't even begun to write an outline for draft number one! And Craig had promised this was easy! It was too late to make an exit, and there were no short cuts. I'd always loathed this way of working, but had to stay calm and abide by the system, as everyone was being supportive and friendly. The main problem by the time we did reach the third draft, was the ABC team insisting my final script was 20 minutes too short. I felt certain it was the right length, but other editors had assessed the timing, and were adamant. With this evidence I gave up protesting. It meant extra scenes, twisting the story into places it was never meant to go. After the final edit, I had a call thanking me for my work. I was told there was just one small problem. Cuts had to be made, as the script was too long. "How long?" I asked. There was a pause. "I'm not supposed to tell you, but it was 20 minutes," she said. It had been an experience, but not one I cared to repeat.

The actor Bill Kerr was one of many Australians who had settled in London. He'd been there for many years, and was a regular in most of the BBC's comedy radio shows. He also played roles in the theatre, which is where Marge and I came to know him. He came back to live in Australia soon after we did, and was cast in a miniseries I wrote called *The Private War Of Lucinda Smith* along with Nigel Havers, Linda Cropper and Vincent Ball. We filmed most of it in Samoa, and in the weeks we were there Bill entertained me with tales of growing up in the southern town of Wagga. It was a bizarre childhood with his stage struck mother, determined young Billy at the age of six, was going to be a star.

With this in mind, she would lend him to any travelling theatrical company who had a role for a child actor, and sometimes weeks later they would send him home by train with a label around his neck: *My name is Bill Kerr. Please put me off at Wagga.*

Eventually she borrowed money, left her husband and moved to Sydney, where she besieged casting directors, fought with producers, and Bill became the six-year-old star of a local Australian film. From then his life consisted of agents and auditions. Out of these conversations came a background of their life in the nineteen thirties, and for me it started to sound like a concept for a screenplay or a novel: a boy growing up in a country town with its tribes and undercurrents, burdened by a mother who was stranded in the town she disliked, and trapped in a failing marriage. Her only passport to the life she craved was her talented small son. All he really wanted was to play with a gang from school. I felt the possibilities of it and began to add fictional elements. By the time we left Samoa I had the idea, with Bill's agreement, for a screenplay. It was motivated by the events of his childhood, but by now he was a different boy and a very different mother. The screenplay was called *The Murrumbidgee Kid*. It is one of my favourite scripts that was never made.

It had keen reactions, not least from Tony Buckley who wrote to me: *one of the best screenplays I've read in a long time, full of nostalgia, pathos, love and most importantly, humour.* Unfortunately we were in that 'anti-nostalgia' decade. So it was read by a long list of people who liked it but didn't acquire it. *The Murrumbidgee Kid* eventually had an important new life when I turned it into a novel. But it was fifteen years before that happened, and other things intervened.

Out of the blue came something I truly wish never happened. There was an offer to write the screenplay of a feature film for the James Davern company, that had an outcome none of us could have predicted. It was a book by Gabrielle Lord called *Whipping Boy*. Had it been a mini-series for television I'd have said no, but since returning home I'd written two forgettable films, and this felt like a chance to do something better. I read the book and found it dark; well-written like all of Gabrielle's work, but concerned with the sick and murky world of a close-knit group of paedophiles. I was not certain I wanted to write the screenplay, but was influenced by the character of Cass Meredith, the lawyer appointed to inquire into child pornography, and the colourful world of eccentrics, transvestites, junkies and others in Kings Cross. It was a good thriller with flashes of humour, and a strong leading role to attract a top female star. All assets for a good feature film. But it was a complex adaptation, a story set in the past and present. As a feature film I felt it had a chance to be a hit, with its shock subject, bizarre characters combined with black humour, but we spent months wrestling with a series of changes. It was also a problem to find a director. My choice was Carl Schultz who didn't like the subject, and turned it down. Several others were approached, and felt nervous about the material. We needed a name actress but could not approach one until a director was in place. It seemed, after two years, as if the script would end up in the graveyard with other films that were never made. I certainly wish it had ended this way. But in 1996, two things happened.

In New South Wales, the Wood Royal Commission into the police force was instigated. In Canberra the Commonwealth government set up a Television Fund, to encourage commercial networks into making more telemovies and miniseries. Channel 10, who had seen the script of *Whipping Boy*, nominated it as their entry for this fund. It was accepted, and after a lot of rewriting, was re-shaped into a movie for television. In the process of adjusting to the small screen, scenes that were expensive had to be cut. Much of the comedy had to be jettisoned, because it was tied to language that would not (at that time) be acceptable on home screens. "Turn off that fucking-excuse-the-French-television", shouts transvestite Loveday Larsen to her daughter, who wasn't really the girl's mum at all, she was really her Dad who'd had a sex operation. Scenes like that got the chop, if you'll forgive the expression. We ended up with what was no more than a routine thriller, despite our best efforts. What might've been a strong film became a weak telemovie. I should have opted out because of the change to television, but since being involved from the start I felt obligated. I also had no idea what lay ahead.

The Wood Commission into the police force had taken a new turn. Paedophilia. It happened when we were filming, and the ugly word seemed to promote lurid evidence, giving credence to the story we were telling about the abuse of children. In the telefilm, and taken directly from Gabrielle's novel, our network of paedophiles included some high profile fictional people. A headmaster of a school, a prominent surgeon and, a Judge of the Supreme Court.

On October 31st, after the film had been shot, edited, and scheduled to be shown in barely a fortnight's time, a backbencher in the New South Wales Legislative Council, (Mrs F. Arena), asked a question about the protection of prominent people by the Wood Commission. She named two. One was my brother, David Yeldham, a Judge of the Supreme Court. I was driving at the time, and heard this on the afternoon radio news. I almost went off the road with shock. We'd always been the closest of brothers. He'd been a constant routine weekend guest before his own marriage. He found us a flat, then a house to rent and eventually to buy. He'd helped us get to England by a guarantee to the tax department, and during all the years away, he forwarded our mail and kept in touch. We'd been friends all our lives but I had no notion of what the newspapers were now calling his 'secret life'. I first heard the phrase when interviewed by the *Herald* journalist Kate McClymont, who seemed to imagine it was known to me. I tried to assure her my surprise was genuine. This secret life, if it existed, apparently meant bisexual activity and could have nothing to do with paedophilia, but during the next few days of uproar and headlines, no-one bothered to make this point clear.

I had to tell David about the imminent program. I dreaded this, but it was essential that he be told, as I knew what the media would make of it. I rang him to explain it was something which could embarrass him, but was pure fiction, based on a novel by another writer, and had been written by her about two years earlier. He accepted it was an unfortunate coincidence, and we talked of Arena's abuse of parliamentary privilege, and the poisonous atmosphere she'd created. David assured me the notion of paedophilia was repellent to him. He felt disgusted, even by implication, that this woman was asserting he could be involved in such a practice. I totally believed him then, and I still do.

But a few days later he committed suicide, and our family's world became a different, very ugly place. His wife and children were besieged by the media with cameras shining flashlights into their windows all night, hoping to tempt an appearance, while taking pictures of the car he'd used to kill himself. I was woken by radio stations requesting interviews, and for the next days our house was under siege with reporters, while the phone rang with requests, sometimes sounding like demands, for more interrogations. The stress was extreme, and there was the additional trauma of knowing in eight days this film would be on the air.

I asked the head of JNP, James Davern, if he could request a delay. Jim did his best, but called me to say there was no way the Ten Network would relinquish this opportunity to cash in. I then asked if my name could be removed from the show. He not only agreed, but insisted the change be done at his company's expense. (I had expected to pay for it.) Although it was arranged, and the film went to air without my credit, the damage was done. Tapes of shows are always sent to newspaper critics long before they appear on air, and in this instance there was no chance they would not connect the names.

The Sydney *Daily Telegraph* used its lurid tabloid headlines to announce David's death across its front page, and on page two told of the extraordinary coincidence, the Judge's brother had written this TV film— about a Judge who was a member of a paedophile network, and not only that, but one of the characters had taken his own life in the same way. It was thoughtless and stupid careless journalism: the Judge in the film had been **murdered** by others in this way, but only those who'd read the book would know this, and the *Telegraph* has never been a paper to bother with corrections. The headlines lasted for weeks. At times we felt it would never go away. We steeled ourselves not to flinch when we opened a newspaper or switched on the news. Since then our family has been strengthened by what we believe to be true; David did have a secret life as a bi-sexual, he knew this was about to be exposed, and could not face family and friends, or, perhaps most of all, his fellow judges with whom he had a regular weekly lunch. He'd hidden it from his twin brother and our family all his life, so how could he face a table of legal friends? His dual sexuality was a shock to all of us, but as one of his nephews said at the family funeral we managed to have without the press: "So he played both sides. What the fuck did it matter? If he'd told us, we could've told him it makes no difference. If he could've told us, indeed. If only he had."

We were deeply moved by messages of support, There were a huge number from friends, also a great many from strangers. These, the ones who sympathised and wanted us to know, were particularly welcome. Our family did suffer. I worried most about the grand-kids who were still young. The school yard is not always a kind place. Most of all I felt admiration for David's widow Anne and her children Bruce, Belinda and James, who hid their grief, and behaved with great dignity.

It occasionally had other impacts. The TV film has thankfully faded into memory, but there were personal incidents. While those at Macmillan were sympathetic, something unexpected occurred. *A Bitter Harvest* was published in March 1997. It was dedicated to Marge, who'd been heavily involved in the research trips, and *to the memory of my brother David*. When there was a second printing the publicity department at Macmillan rang to say I'd been asked to appear on the *Midday Show*. There was much excitement as this program had a huge audience and it would obviously help book sales. The producer of the show rang to discuss details of my appearance. Eventually he came to the main reason for his call. "We'll plug the book," he promised, "but of course the main part of the interview will be about your brother." I appreciated his honesty, but told him to forget it.

I couldn't and wouldn't do it. There was no way I'd use an interview about David's death to sell books. Declining to go on the *Midday Show* was accepted by Cate and others at Pan Macmillan, but it upset a few people. One in particular was disappointed and said it was a bad career move. I kept my mouth shut, but it was difficult.

*****

Later that year Marge and I went back to London for six weeks. Friends John and Judy Barry were in Switzerland, so they kindly offered us their Belgravia apartment. We caught up with Beryl, Bob Banks-Stewart and other English friends, had a trip down the Nile, then headed for Sussex to see Carl and Julia Schultz, now living in Britain.

In 1956, when it was under Russian rule, Carl escaped from Hungary. He provided me with background of how it had been during that time in Budapest, as my next book was to be about the post war influx of migrants, when Australia's slogan had been 'populate or perish'. I wanted to write about it ever since being impressed by Sir Raphael Cilento, who spent his time aiding Displaced Persons, and when asked why, gave this answer to the United Nations: *Because they sit upon the conscience of the world.*

I had nothing yet on paper, just thoughts of two main characters; a Hungarian brother and sister who had managed to hide from the Nazis, then had to escape when the Russians took over. There were two other vital characters, a German woman survivor of Belsen and an English soldier who rescues her when his unit reaches the death camp. After discharge he is employed by the UN refugee organisation, and is a link between the other main characters. I had no advanced plot, except knowing the four would end up in Australia, part of the great diaspora who had spent years in refugee camps, desperate to find a country when most nations did not want them. I'd met some like that on the Snowy, the year before we went to England, and knew the Hungarian brother and sister would be sent to work there.

It was called *Against The Tide*, the third book since turning to period and historic novels. Pan Macmillan provided an effective cover. It showed people on a crowded boat clutching shabby suitcases, gazing nervously at the shore as if wondering what kind of future they'd have. For those who came here this anxiety was verified. It was the largest population growth in our history. Over two million refugees left their ruined countries to start a new life. They'd been promised paradise, but in that xenophobic epoch they rarely found it. Most arrived to find they were called 'reffos' or worse. Billeted in army huts, forced by government contract to work on manual jobs for two years, no matter what qualifications they possessed, their welcome was often met with indifference or abuse. Despite this hostile reception many went on to achieve great things, and helped to change this country for the better.

I'm often asked which is my favourite book, and this one goes close. My son considers it the best. It was certainly written from the heart. I'd briefly been a newcomer in another country, and knew the feeling.

The next and last book I wrote for Pan Macmillan began through a casual remark at a dinner table. My brother-in-law, Alex Faure, was French, but born in Japan where he grew up. When the Pacific war began he was just eighteen years old, and fortunately saved from internment because the French, after being conquered by Hitler, were considered to be neutral foreigners. Because of this he was able to live under restraint in Yokohama or Tokyo. There were difficulties, food shortages and all neutrals had to report to the police each month. Not a great deal of fun was our opinion, but it provoked a comment from his wife Winifred, who said, "No fun? You should hear more about what he got up to during the war."

We knew it was almost impossible for a foreigner to obtain work in those years, but Winifred reminded us that Alex spoke French, English and Japanese, and this brought him a job in Tokyo with the Banque de l'Indo Chine, The French Bank, as it was called. There he experienced four years of an adventurous life. It contained some serious danger, some humour as well, and in addition rather a lot of sex.

Since Alex sat smiling and saying little, we suggested they come and stay for the weekend. I put a tape recorder on a table between us, and let him talk. From this meeting and others, gradually came a story of a boy aged 18 to 21, becoming a key figure in the dangerous task of sending currency to banks in Switzerland. It meant a risky life dispatching millions in the diplomatic bag that went via Paris, while escaping scrutiny of the secret police, the dreaded *Kempetai*. Suspicion could mean imprisonment, proof would have brought a death sentence. Throughout the worst of the war, when American planes were blitzing Tokyo, Alex lived in the Ginza occupying a tiny apartment on the top floor of the bank where, despite the bombing, he managed to have a busy love life. We eventually got to hear about some of the romantic moments, and finally I sat down to write about his war from all the material he'd eventually given me. I called it *Land Of Dreams*.

It was a story too good to ignore, and I finished the book and sent it to Cate Paterson at Pan Macmillan. She surprised me by rejecting it on the grounds that it had no links with Australia. A strange comment, I thought, but it seemed I was now classified by *A Bitter Harvest* and stuck with the 'Australian blockbuster' tag. Flattering as it sounded, I did not want to be tied to that description. It was also my first rejection since *Reprisal* had done the rounds, and it felt like a slap in the face.

I'd wasted a year, and to me it contained a wealth of material that had never been told before, including extra research I'd gathered at the Japanese reference library in North Sydney. I felt it should be used somehow, so gave the manuscript to John Croyston, who read it and suggested, "Could Alex maybe have a relative in Australia?" It was a very clever solution.

John and his wife Janet were now neighbors, having moved to the central coast, and it was his comment that gave me the answer. I'd written it as a factual story, but with Alex's agreement it could become part fiction. An important character could have some affiliation with Australia. He could, as John said, have a relative. Alex agreed, because he wanted the book published. He had friends still in Japan, others who had migrated to America, as well as relations in France, all of whom had heard about the book and were wanting to have a copy. So the new version went ahead, a youngish aunt was introduced, and through her eyes we saw much of Australia's war on the home front; the barbed wire on beaches, the censorship, Sydney's submarine attack, and the bombing of Darwin. It was a major reconstruction taking several months.

The result? I sent the rewrite to Cate who promptly accepted this version, which was published in 2002. It read well, but I was never pleased at having to distort the true story to get it into bookshops. I think after the first flush of interest from friends and relatives they felt the same. I was regretful of the compromise, and twelve years later the factual version was republished under a new title, *Dragons In The Forest*. It came about through another publisher, but to be honest, from this distance I think Cate was right. Out of interest I read both versions again recently, and feel *Land of Dreams* is a better and more exciting book to read, being able to involve a youth barely out of school, not only undergoing the dangers in wartime Japan, but managing to keep in touch with his Aussie aunt despite the suspicion and close scrutiny of a secret policeman determined to trap him.

It was the last book I wrote for Pan Macmillan, and I'm still not quite sure why we drifted apart. It was a strange time, after such good rapport with Cate that produced five books. I don't know why, but I was feeling uncomfortable there. Perhaps it was the drama of my switch from the kind of books they'd expected me to write. Or the turning down of the *Midday Show*. I had no regrets, even though I wondered, as writers tend to do, if this was the end of the line. That was when Anthony Buckley called, asking me to adapt Bryce Courtenay's latest book *Jessica* for television.

This was a good strong story, one of Bryce's best, but through no fault of his it proved to be a long and testing delay. From the time I signed a contract with Screentime, who owned the rights, until the day filming began, there was a gap that extended more than four years, a period that tested all of us in various ways. Bryce got fed up with the procrastination and secretly spoke to me about threatening not to not renew the option. Tony Buckley was upset, and Tony is noted in the business for his courtesy and patience, but he felt the budget was inadequate. My complaint was an irritating lack of courtesy, something I had never encountered anywhere before; Screentime and the Channel Ten executives were having conferences about the script without inviting the writer to attend. So while waiting for them to get their act together, I spent the four years writing two quite different novels. Both, in time, became important.

One, like much in life, happened by chance. Perry and Mary Anne were on a tour of the battlefields in France. They were accompanying her father, and following the footsteps of her grandfather who had been at Pozieres and other towns along the Somme. Marge and I were in London, when Perry phoned to suggest we take the Eurostar to join them.

"You never know, Dad," he said, "there might be something worthwhile over here." It was an understatement. The first day, in Villers Bretonneux, we heard the infant schoolchildren start their morning by singing *Waltzing Matilda*, a beautiful sound in the French language. Their youthful voices seemed to be paying tribute to the Anzac counter-attack that saved their town, nearly a hundred years earlier. We were shown the school's huge sign across their tennis court that said: *Don't Forget Australia*. I was astonished how many towns in northern France had tributes to the Anzacs. There were streets with Australian names. Everywhere we saw affection for the troops who had fought there. In the well-kept cemeteries were the headstones, rows of Aussie soldiers, who are, the inscriptions says, "known only to God." It was in one of these immaculate memorial grounds, filled with so many nameless patriots, that I started to think about a book. Before leaving France I knew I'd write it.

At home weeks later, my mind was full of questions about it, starting with the search for a main character. So much of the story must revolve about him. Was he a country lad from the bush? A high percentage of recruits had come from small towns, where pressure to join up was acute. Would he be forced like some, to enlist or face white feathers and taunts of cowardice? No, I discarded that. He'd be typical of those swept up by martial music and recruiting rallies, where politicians were eagerly persuading young men to sign up and do their bit for the Empire.

He would fight in Gallipoli and France. Particularly France. We still venerate Gallipoli, but more time was spent along the Somme where so many of our soldiers fought and died. By now I felt my character would be nineteen, a first year law student, who leaves University to join up. I spent a lot of time thinking about the central character. It's never an easy process, this first step, because if you get the wrong character you can waste weeks, or even become discouraged and abandon it. Nostalgically I named him Stephen Conway, making him a distant descendent of the Conway family, echoes of Bess and Jeremy, who had been a favourite mum and dad in my memory.

Like many recruits, Stephen volunteered partly out of patriotism, but also with thoughts of adventure. I felt this was a motive for some enlistments. It was a time when only the rich could afford travel, and here was a chance to wear the uniform and see the world. They were told, and most believed, that the war would certainly be over by Christmas. No-one could imagine it would last four years. Survivors with battle fatigue and shell shock surely felt betrayed by those who'd promised them such a quick and easy victory.

That was how this book started. A brief holiday with my son and daughter-in-law, touring a district where towns have been rebuilt, where cattle now graze in lush acres, and it is difficult to believe millions died, until you see the graveyards. I spent most of a year writing it, and no longer wanting to approach Pan Macmillan, I sent it to Random House. Months passed without a word from them. In the end I had to write requesting they return the manuscript. Discouraged, I put it in the bottom drawer, out of sight. In my mind by then I'd consigned it to the dustbin, never expecting to resume work on it. How wrong can you be! It became the book everyone remembers.

There was still delay on the production of *Jessica*. Two drafts had been written before I even met with director, Peter Andrikidis, and most of the notes I received for script changes kept coming from conferences held without me being present. Screentime paid reasonable fees, but their treatment left a lot to be desired.

So with time to spare I had a look at another project, the one I'd hoped would be a film. Tony Buckley had been so keen on the script of *The Murrumbidgee Kid*, that his comments made me think. If not a film, I could try it as a novel.

That was when, for the first time, I had what is known as writer's block. I could not progress the story for weeks—until I found the reason why. I was adapting my own screenplay to become a book, and it was a mistake. The novel had to be approached differently. So I burnt all my notes, and began again. It was surprising how it freed the process. I concentrated on the boy who just wants to be one of the kids in the playground, and his mother who takes him far away from the Murrumbidgee, into a celluloid world. I fortunately finished it just before word came that *Jessica* was at last ready to go.

This meant a busy time. It meant a third draft script with another bundle of notes from the numerous executives that annoyed me. In a long career, this was the only time I'd been given so many script suggestions, without an invitation to be at the meetings where they'd emanated. This last bundle was over the top; sent by email the day of a final gathering, with Tony and Bryce Courtenay, along with Peter Andrikidis, and other members of the Screentime company in attendance at Yarramalong. Bryce was asked for his opinion of the script, and was very complimentary, telling us he did not want there to be any changes. That was when I had to point out the bundle of notes I'd received. It had arrived by email only that morning.

"A bit late for more note surely. How many notes?" Bryce wanted to know.

"Rather a lot," I said.

"How many is a lot," he asked.

"I haven't had time for a count, Bryce, as this only arrived less than an hour ago, but the note with it said there are seventy suggested changes." I saw the stunned faces on some of the gathering. "A few," the note said, "are quite small.."

"Jesus Christ, the last thing this script needs is any changes. Small or miniscule. Tear up the fucking email and the bloody notes with them."

Tony Buckley was vocally in agreement. So was the director, and if anyone was in support of an examination of the suggestions, they remained silent. Two weeks later filming began at last. The finished product was shown to all the cast and crew at theatre belonging to Film Australia. It looked good. Leeanna Walsman as Jessica, was brilliant. So was Sam Neill, as the congenial and drunken lawyer. When it was shown on Channel Ten, four and a half years had elapsed since I sat down to write the first line of draft one. I was glad to see the end of it. Not because of the book. *Jessica* was a good story. In addition we had fine actors, and Australia's best producer. But there were other executives. Too many chiefs, who, by their attitude, made me feel like the only Indian.

The Logies are a show-biz event that seem to carry a great deal of credence. It is not, and never has been, my idea of a good night out. When I adapted the miniseries *1915* for the ABC it won this award, but since then I've never attended or watched this ceremony. So I had no idea that *Jessica* had been nominated or short listed. Not until Mireille, my French sister-in-law phoned me with congratulations.

"For what?" I asked.

"The Logie," she said, surprised I didn't know. "Both the Logies."

It turned out *Jessica* had been declared the year's best miniseries and Sam Neill had won the award as best male actor. In his speech Sam apparently thanked both Tony and me, which was how Mireille knew. Nobody had even bothered to mention to me it had been nominated. It was with sheer amazement I later gathered not even Tony Buckley had been present. He should have been there accepting the award, which was for some reason given to Greg Haddrick instead. The show had also apparently won an award in Chicago the previous year, but that hadn't been mentioned either. There was something very strange about the whole thing. Tony was clearly invited, but apparently invitations went in different directions, and he was tricked out of being present. He was angry and upset, with very good cause to be so. I sent my script to the National Archive with some caustic remarks that guaranteed the company would never again wish me to work for them. By choice it was the last time I wrote a television script for anyone. From then on, I preferred novels. But I didn't write much at all that year. Other events made it impossible.

It is sometimes difficult to remember the precise date when the worst kind of things happen. It was in 2003, a night when Marge had a bad fall on the way to dinner. Part of a stone stairway gave way and she fell down the rough steps; it was a nasty accident leaving her bruised and shaken. X-rays proved she'd fractured several ribs. I drove her to our local doctor the next morning and waited until asked to join them, to hear the X-rays had revealed a shadow on her lungs. It was almost certainly cancer. Life changes after a statement like that. I can only recall Marjorie's wry remark that it was unfair—she'd given up smoking many years ago, long before all of us.

We went home trying to reassure each other there'd be treatment; at least the fall she'd had was lucky, for the cancer was revealed in the early stages. That's if it really was cancer. So far it was just a shadow on the X-Ray, no proof it was malignant. We were to see a Professor who would carry out more tests, but we couldn't get an appointment for at least two weeks. I thought it incredible we had to wait so long; I knew if it was me I'd go raving mad having to even wait a day.

But Marge was outwardly calm. Even when the Professor did confirm it was positive, she tried to accept it with equanimity. Next there came a choice of oncologists, after that we attended the first day of chemotherapy. It was a clinical room at North Gosford hospital, where all the patients seemed to know each other. There were a few women there wearing head scarves or beanies. Marge decided if she lost her hair she'd insist on a bright red wig. Later that day the nurse in charge announced one of her patients was cured, and would not be back. All the patients applauded this lucky person.

The staff were kind; there was morning tea and lunch. It was to be a constant routine for many months, treatment each week, and sickness the next few days, until at last there was a break from chemotherapy. We went to Norfolk Island, renting a car and a cottage. It was idyllic, finding beautiful places like Quality Row and historic Emily Beach. Marge was relaxed, determined a few spots on her lung were not going to change her way of living, and happy so far, that she had not lost her hair.

When the chemo continued to make her sick we sought other ways. In quiet desperation we went to consult a leading surgeon who said unfortunately an operation was not feasible. There was another stretch of chemo, then we had a trip to Tasmania. It was impossible to go on long journeys; Europe for instance, where friends were emailing us to come and stay, was just too far. I knew she secretly wanted to revisit London, but we couldn't go because of the shortness between treatments, and the length of the flight. Instead we took the car to Tasmania on the ferry, spent time with my brother Dick, who now lives there, and also met up with Di Drew, another resident, who brilliantly directed the Anzac scenes in my adaptation of Roger McDonald's book *1915*.

We came back on the ferry to Melbourne, intending to drive along the Murray, then head to Broken Hill. But at Mildura I got an attack of giddiness that turned out to be vertigo, so Broken Hill was abandoned. Marge said I needed to see a doctor, and as my eyesight was affected, she insisted on driving us all the way back to Sydney.

After a time the chemo treatments caused further complications; they upset her immune system, lowering her white cell count, so she needed regular blood transfusions instead of chemo. For these treatments she drove herself to the hospital, determined to remain independent. Whenever anyone asked the cliché question, "How are you", her instinctive reply was "Fine." But of course she wasn't fine. Just determined and wonderfully brave.

She insisted that I go back to work, wanting me to improve *Murrumbidgee Kid* or the book set in France that was still called *Finding Stephen*. Both these novels were sitting uselessly on my desk, both still needing final work. I decided to tackle *Murrumbidgee* first. It was through adapting *Jessica* that I became close friends with Bryce Courtenay. We spent a lot of time together while the filming took place, and after it was over he bought a block of land and built a house at the end of our valley. We often saw him after that. I'd just done a final polish on *Murrumbidgee Kid*, when we met at a dinner party given by painter David Voigt and his wife Pia. Bryce asked what I was doing. Was I going back to television?

No thanks, I said. We'd both had a rough ride on *Jessica*, with the frequent changes and long delays. I told him I'd written a new book, but was unsure what to do with it. It'd been a bad year with Marge's illness, and I lacked confidence, feeling the book was a candidate for the bottom drawer, until Bryce asked if he could read some chapters. I gave him the whole manuscript of *The*

Bryce Courtenay with Peter at the launch of The Murrumbidgee Kid.

Marge and Peter in 2005.

Murrumbidgee Kid which he read the following week, and unknown to me, sent it to Bob Sessions, the senior publisher at Penguin.

It was almost Christmas when Bob rang to say it was being considered, but not to expect a quick answer because of the summer holidays. But just two weeks later, barely January, came the news he and Ali Watts liked it very much, and wanted to publish. It was like a delayed but splendid yuletide gift that began a new chapter in my life. Penguin felt exciting, and full of enthusiasm about the book. It was launched at Bryce's house in the valley, giving me a chance to pay some tributes.

"My thanks to Penguin publishers Julie Gibbs and Robert Sessions who have come from Melbourne to be here today. To Ali Watts who said yes. To Saskia Adams, who agreed. My special gratitude to Bryce for his friendship and hosting us here today, and thank you all for coming.

Which leaves just one more person to thank. She's survived many years of radio and television scripts, screenplays, stage plays, and finally novels. It's been a long and happy partnership of shared humour and love. So thank you Marge, I couldn't have done it without you."

There was a real feeling of camaraderie about Penguin that was infectious, something I hadn't experienced until then. Each week Saskia kept in touch to inform me how well the book was selling. Ali Watts and Saskia Adams wrote welcoming letters that are attached to correspondence at the end of this book.

Meanwhile I was working on a new draft of the novel set in the 1914-18 war on the Somme that was still being called *Finding Stephen*. I'd felt it was not strong enough and had lumbered it with a sub-plot. Ali and Saskia disagreed, as a result here were a lot of notes from them leading to a massive rewrite over the next six months. But it was well worth it; their revisions strengthened the story immensely. I also found a lot of additional research that was exciting and introduced the hitherto unknown website

SHOT AT DAWN, with its appalling record of the many English soldiers shot for what were often merely trifling offences.

Over 1500 British and Empire soldiers were executed by their own side in that war. Not a single Australian faced a firing squad. The government refused to allow it because all our troops were volunteers, not conscripts. The clash between both countries over this was a highlight incident, and one of the core conflicts newly introduced in the book. It became a ferocious dispute between Whitehall and Canberra over the fate of one man. When the revised version was finished everyone liked the result, but I was the only one who still liked the title. There were many suggestions for a change, most of them rapidly rejected, then one day Perry sent me an email with just four words: *BARBED WIRE AND ROSES*. I promptly sent it to Ali who instantly emailed, 'that's it!' So the book that began with my son's suggestion that we come to France, went to print soon after he provided the new title.

It was certainly my most admired novel. For years emails poured in from people who identified with this story of an adventurous youth, who'd ended up in the nightmare of trench warfare, and how, at another current level, it involved the search by his grandson about what happened to him, because he was not listed among the dead, nor did he ever come home again

Like all my work Marge had a lot of input into *Barbed Wire and Roses*. But she didn't live to see it published. She died in September 2006 after three weeks in hospital. The first week, the attending doctor said it would only be a matter of days. The second week he told my son and daughter their mother was an amazing fighter, and might even be able to return to her own bed. But soon her immune system could not cope, and she died peacefully after the three of us spent all night at her bedside.

A lot of people came to say goodbye. Lyn spoke, so did Perry and our grandson Pete. I found it difficult, but here is part of what I said.

Thank you all for coming. I hope you'll join us afterwards because that was a wish Marge once expressed to me. There should always be a time to talk, she said, to mingle and remember, then everyone can get on with the rest of their lives.
For three years she fought a battle against lung cancer, and when the chemo destroyed her immune system she endured a weekly blood transfusion, and set out to live a normal life, driving herself to the hospital for chemo and later transfusions. She never cried, never whinged, even on the worst days. If she was asked how she felt she had an unfailing reply. "I'm fine". She always said it, sometimes baffled doctors, unused to hearing that response from patients. "I'm fine" I can still hear her saying it. I'll always hear it.
Marge had a studio upstairs in our house. She had a studio in every house we lived in, full of paint brushes and easels, of stained glass and tools she used to create windows and lamp shades. She was never at a loss, never bored. There was always a project, always music playing.
We've been together a long time. Married over fifty years, we became used to incredulous looks. One marriage, all that time! What did you talk about? I can tell you, we never ran out of things to say. We laughed and loved, and fought now and then, but never for long. All our lives we were a partnership, in every sense of the word. We shared the early days when we were broke, the decisions that seemed a bit crazy at the time, like taking our kids to England with no return fares.
We met on the 27th of August 1947, she reminded me just the other day. It was the most fortuitous day of my life, just as last Monday was the saddest. But as she said to Lyn, Perry and me, "No tears, my darlings". Well, it's not easy, my darling, but we'll try to do as you wish. And if asked how we are, we'll try to say "We're fine. Just fine."

There were messages from overseas that Lyn read out. Vincent Ball, speaking of the glass paintings she gave as presents said: "There's a touch of Marge in all our houses."

Rod Milgate wrote her a beautiful poem that ended: *Shadows will not engulf that lovely face.*

And there were many phone calls, cards and emails from overseas and interstate. Letters kept coming for weeks afterwards. And following the memorial service our house was filled with people who had been her friends. She would have been very glad of that.

*****

PART TEN: LONELY YEARS

I stayed in our same house for almost seven more years, often debating about a move. But the daunting idea of fitting into a modest city apartment after downsizing, disposing of half the furniture and most of the books, and giving up a home we'd lived in far longer than any other made me baulk at leaving. I baulked because it contained twenty years of fond memories, but every morning the loneliness grew.

I found it difficult to write at all without Marjorie. She never liked her full name, saying her parents called her that when she was young and misbehaved. Our long life together had been part of a pattern; sometimes discussing ideas, talking of how things were progressing, asking her to read parts of a book or a script when I had doubts; other times, just going up to her studio, to chat while she worked on a glass lamp shade or a brilliantly coloured window. If I had problems with what I was writing, she quite often had solutions. It made me realise how much she'd contributed, ever since we'd combined to think of plots for that first break-through radio series *Two Stars and a Story*. It had been, in every sense of the word, a partnership. If you take that interaction for granted, you miss it desperately when it is no longer there.

I missed it every single day. I missed knowing she was upstairs creating whichever of her projects was current; I missed the distant sound of her music, either a record of one of the recent musicals, or her playing the piano, the flute, or her guitar. I missed the tap on my shoulder around six o'clock, when there was a glass of wine. For months I kept thinking of things I wanted to tell her, before the acceptance it was not possible, and never would be again. Moments like that can bring you close to futile tears.

Settling down to write again was a hard task. For weeks it seemed impossible. In the end I was assisted by Penguin. Months earlier they'd asked all their authors to write a piece for an anthology called *How We Met*. This description of how writers had found their partners was published as a fundraiser for Pen International, who supported writers around the world. I hadn't yet written it, and they no longer expected a contribution, but I felt it might help. It did, evoking a flow of memories. Penguin seemed pleased with it; more importantly I gave copies to my son and daughter, and treasured their replies. *It's absolutely beautiful*, Lyn said. *Truly beautiful. It makes me sad, yet very happy at the same time. A lot of your soul in this*, was Perry's reply.

My version of *How We Met* was published the following year along with about twenty other writers, and made me feel ready to tackle something new. No novel as yet; I couldn't face the schedule of working late nights in the empty house. That was when Tony Buckley and I began looking for a new project. Tony found a challenging book that we felt would make a great film. It was a Miles Franklin winner, Thea Astley's novel *Drylands*. He took an option on it, I wrote a script, and Bruce Beresford was going to direct. It felt positive, but, with all our experience, and Tony and Bruce making several of the finest Australian movies, our application for finance was rejected. We had an acrimonious meeting with the funding body, but that was the end of it. After days like that I felt it was easier to deal with film studios in the UK, or even America, than tackle factions in Australia. There are sometimes undercurrents in these cliques. Too much previous history of amity or perhaps enmity. I remember how we left that meeting stunned and angry, feeling it had not been a fair hearing, and would've been a very worthwhile film.

With the film blocked, time began to drag. Living alone was not proving easy and I needed to occupy the empty days. I remembered a tragic event six years earlier, when an Indonesian fishing boat sank drowning 300 asylum seekers, many of them children. I'd kept a news clipping with a photo of three Iraqi sisters among the dead, their ages six, seven and nine. They were lovely children; the picture of them motivated me to write about the government's harsh treatment of people who were fleeing from tyranny in their attempt to find refuge. For some reason I kept thinking of two national leaders, and their divergent words.

John F. Kennedy: "Ask not what your country can do for you, ask what you can do for your country."

John Howard: "We will decide who comes to this country, and the manner in which they come."

This led to a book that I set in the year when Howard said this, a time of cruelty, government lies and overcrowded detention centres. A time when an election was fought over the arrival of boats, and votes were won or lost on the issue of preventing them. It was a book I relished writing, as it not only expressed my views, but also because of its spirited characters. It began with Katerina, a Greek girl who arrives in Australia aged six, abruptly abandoned there by her wayward mother who has had a love affair with a member of the crew and goes back with him to Athens, leaving her daughter with an estranged father whom she hardly knows. Her childhood is at first a battleground, facing school each day where she's ignored or teased for being a foreigner. Katerina survives it, she makes friends and becomes better known as Kate. In her teens she joins in protests against the Vietnam war. After a youthful love affair ends badly, she joins a firm run by a lawyer assisting refugees. Until one night, a moment of compassion to help a run-away child makes her violate the rigorous laws, and changes her life forever.

Bryce Courtenay is quoted on the front page how much he loved the book, as much as I did. The main characters, Damien and Kate, as well as her eccentric Greek mother, Sofia, are among my favourites, while the endearing Uncle Angelo and Aunt Fanny, based on two Italian relatives of our own family, and vividly recalled by my cousin John Clements, were an absolute joy to write. When you get characters like that, it's a pleasure to start work each day. I wanted to call it Katerina, as she is the main figure throughout this book, but my low record with titles continued as it ended up being called *A Distant Shore*. I felt this was a title used before, but despite that the book created interest. I have a box full of emails from readers, a few of which can be found attached to the back of this book. When I came to select them, I was surprised how many readers had written giving generous praise to *A Distant Shore*. They outnumbered all other books including *Barbed War and Roses*. It was encouraging; at a time when politicians were trying to win votes by locking up asylum seekers, people were buying and praising a book that disparaged the treatment of refugees, dismissing them with epithets like 'boat people.'

While writing that book, a thought occurred to me. All of us, except the original owners, either came here or are descended from ancestors who arrived by ship. But today's slogan that wins elections is the cruel crusade launched by the words **stop the boats**. Had the original owners enforced this attitude with the ferocity of today's politicians, none of us might be living here.

One weekend morning I woke up feeling ill, and my daughter drove me to hospital. Apart from the interminable wait in emergency,

I can't remember what happened next. It was apparently a perforated gallbladder. I was moved to Gosford Hospital, underwent an operation, and have no recollection of the following ten days I spent in intensive care. It was a wonderful relief from the dark confusing nightmares to hear familiar voices, then see the faces of my son and daughter at the bedside. They'd apparently spent days there, but I'd been unaware, and could hardly believe it. Even now I wanted to be sure this was real, that it was really them. The nightmares had been a strange torment that seemed to be telling me I'd never see them again. Later, when they had gone after promises they'd be back the next day, I looked out a window to see drifting clouds, and I asked a nurse to open the curtain wider, so I could be sure they were real clouds gliding across a real sky. She looked at me as if wondering about my state of mind, and I tried to explain that it was an odd feeling to want proof of being alive, no longer in the grip of darkness and delusion. I don't think my explanation convinced her. I got some curious looks from her and other nurses for the next few days in the intensive ward, until I was dispatched to an ordinary ward, and then the day when the glad sight of Vincent Ball arrived to drive me home.

Having been healthy most of my adult life, this was an abrupt change. The next year I needed a back operation, and not long afterwards another, which made it difficult to look after the grassy paddocks at Yarramalong. Back pains started to tell me it was time to give up using a tractor, or even a ride-on mower. So, with some regret, I put the place on the market. It would mean leaving many good friends who lived there, like Liz and Peter Lawson who go back to schooldays, and recent mates Pia and David Voigt, Lorraine and Greg Woon, as well as neighbours Jo and Laurie Eyes, and Vince Ball, who since being the chauffeur who drove me home, resumed his phone calls each week, asking if I was in for coffee, and turning up as he had done for years, to discuss our health and any new medical reports.

Buying the house and its ten acres had been an instant decision; selling it proved a far slower process. It stayed on the market for over two years, with property in the district affected because of a threat to start coal mining in the Yarramalong Valley. We all joined a local campaign against it, believing we had the support of Barry O'Farrell, then leader of the state Liberal party. He not only attended protest meetings and gave assurances in the press, he was even photographed in t-shirts containing slogans to convince everyone of his loyalty in the forthcoming state election. But as promises become forgotten after election day, he retracted all of his, and because of this political chicanery the threat of a coal mine and the difficulty of selling property remained. Apart from cheering when he was disposed, I could not cut the grass or sell the house, so I started a new book.

Glory Girl was a blend of fiction with the factual story of aviators Bill Lancaster and Jessie Miller, who attempted to make a record flight from London to Australia in a light aircraft. The year was 1927, and no-one had ever done it. I first heard of them from expatriate Wylton Dickson, who researched their lives, and suggested I write their story as a new miniseries for television. Titled *The Lancaster-Miller Affair*, it was shown on the Nine Network creating interest with historian Graham Ramsay, and Craig Munro, author of the award-winning *Wild Men of Letters* and a publisher at the University of Queensland Press. Craig asked me to write the story as a book at that time. We had some meetings to discuss it, but caught up with the task of writing the James Cook screenplay, and the long battle to get it produced, I reluctantly had to decline his offer.

I always had regrets, but 25 years later I felt able to contemplate it as a book again, but since it was no longer authentic history, it could be a book with a wider canvas. Their flight and the murder trial were facts in the public domain and essential, but beyond that, Jessie Miller's early life in particular, was unknown. It allowed me the freedom to expand her story, giving Jessie a new name and background. The emphasis is on her, the main character who has a life before the two fliers ever meet. She runs away from an unhappy home in the outback of Western Australia, finds a job in Melbourne, then migrates to London. There she has a love affair with an Aussie journalist who works in Fleet Street, and he becomes an integral part of the book, recounting much of their story.

It received warm praise at Penguin. Saskia Adams, still my editor there, enthused. She declared it my best book. It was commended as a *Christina Stead Award* by the Fellowship of Australian Writers. In addition it was given a special sticker—*Guaranteed great read or your money back*—which Penguin considered their ultimate compliment, but to me always felt needlessly rash. I'm not sure if readers took advantage and got their money back, or if it had disappointing results. It was about then I lost touch with Saskia, who always advised me on sales. When emails went unanswered I gave up, puzzled at this after seven years of what had been a presumed friendship.

The house was still unsold. I found a new estate agent, and settled down to concentrate on a new novel. It was a wartime and post-war story about a group of friends who grow up on the northern beaches. The central characters, Luke and Claudia, fall in love until separated by the war. Their circle of friends disintegrate, as Luke becomes a leading journalist overseas, writing books and returning when Britain conducts nuclear tests in Western Australia. He risks freedom by exposing what follows at Maralinga, when the very secret and illegal trials are carried out. This book took nearly two years, rewriting the mix of friendships and loving relationships among the group. Ali Watts was enthusiastic. A new estate agent produced a possible buyer for the house, a nice couple with three children. Everything was looking promising until the phone rang. It was a call from Melbourne, Ali Watts with news that reduced me to a state of shock. Penguin had rejected the book. Ali was also in shock as she had started to edit it, asking me to make some minor changes, unaware the number-crunchers would meet and reject it. She was deeply apologetic, and the manuscript was returned with a letter that revealed her dismay. She was kind enough to suggest other publishers, as rejection meant I wouldn't want to write for Penguin again.

This kick in the teeth came a few days before I'd been asked to speak about the next book at the Tuggerah library, one of my favourite places. The staff were friends, and I'd launched several books there. I thought of cancelling the appearance, then decided to hell with that, so I turned up, outlined the story and all the highlights to this responsive audience, then startled them with news of its rejection. Amid the sympathy came a request that if and when I found another publisher, to please return there and launch it.

Alone at home afterwards I was not so sanguine, facing what was a savage blow that left me feeling shattered. Another irony, by then the house sale was settled and signed; it was time to start packing. Lyn had found a perfect three bedroom, ground floor apartment near the station in Wollstonecraft and moving began to take over from grievance. Half a lifetime of clutter went to St Vinnie's or the local tip. A few hundred books went to charities and the restored Yarramalong library. Lyn organised a garage sale for the remaining clutter. I moved to Sydney in 2013, lucky to have a caring family with daughter, son and daughter-in-law, who all helped in this relocation. So did Lyn's husband, Rod, who spent days drilling the walls of the new flat in order to hang paintings and photographs. At the time neither he nor we realised it, but he was diagnosed with cancer, and sadly died in August that year. Their daughter Olivia, and her husband Michael, flew from London so the family could be with him during those final weeks.

*****

PART ELEVEN: WOLLSTONECRAFT

In Wollstonecraft, before moving in, we measured bookcases and the main furniture to find out what would fit in the apartment. First and foremost my antique desk, acquired one fortunate day on the top floor of Harrods, where they hide the period pieces and other treasures. On it has been written every word since 1966 when it arrived to replace the old table I'd worked on in London. It was where I sat down in 2013 to revise *Friends or Lovers,* as the book was then called, acutely aware this was no easy to time to find another publisher, with redundancies and reports of closing bookshops.

I kept thinking of the irony; I'd started to write at seventeen, and was now on the brink of eighty seven. Almost exactly seventy years since the days of running messages at 2GB. Was it time to quit? Try to play golf again? Not possible with my crook back. What about bowls? No thanks. I posted the manuscript to a British literary agent who'd asked to read it. Nine months later she wrote to say how much she liked it. I replied to thank her for the interest, but explained the news was a bit too late.

Her letter arrived in July 2014, and I'd met with a new publisher in January.

Since moving to Sydney, the trauma of rejection had begun to diminish. This new publisher was Jennifer McDonald and her firm was called *For Pity Sake*. A tribute to her father, Keith McDonald, she said, when I asked its origin. Keith had been the previous Head of Queensland Newspapers, and the father of four daughters This was a familiar phrase from their youth Jenny explained, often directed at her and her three sisters in moments of uproar or family stress.

Friends or Lovers was revised by me, edited by her, and renamed by my son. No-one, apart from me, liked the old title. Perry, being a journalist all his working life, supplied the new words on the cover. *Above The Fold* is a term that denotes the section of a broadsheet newspaper, where the main stories are found. It fitted the character of Luke and was published in November 2014. A full house at the Tuggerah library was there at the launch, and Ali Watts wrote to wish me well. Nothing like that came from anyone else at Penguin.

Gabrielle Lord and Nicole Alexander both read it. Gabrielle called it, *A big hearted novel that examines emotions of love and loyalty.* Nicole wrote, *An engaging story.*

After twenty years in Yarramalong it was the start of a very different way of life, alone in a comfortable apartment on the edge of the city. Living closer to both children and the growing grandkids was a pleasure, but I did miss what I'd taken for granted, like the forest surround, the peaceful acreage, and in summer the swimming pool. People who move a lot, like we did in both countries, develop a deep affection for certain homes we inhabit. It only happened twice, and each time it was a wrench, but in England there were two of us to share the feeling of leaving The Oaks. Here the time occupied was far longer, and although I grew impatient at the time selling it took, I knew I was going to regret leaving. The block of flats in Wollstonecraft had a pleasant and colourful garden, but it wasn't mine. I look back on nearly six years of time, and realise a lot of it was spent inside, writing.

Jennifer's firm published two more of my books. One was not strictly new. It was the original story of my brother-in-law, Alex Faure. Some major revision was done, but in essence it was the account of his life as a neutral foreigner in Japan during the war, the version Pan Mac did not want because it lacked any mention of Australia. This revealed the story of how he lived through the war and survived massive bombing raids on Tokyo, while taking risks to support his family.

It was a more truthful book. I'd always had some regret for agreeing to write a fictional version, which was certainly more lively, and with Alex's co-operation written in the style of a thriller, but I'd long felt it essential the correct story of his life and exploits during the war should really be told. Finance was a problem, so I agreed to fund the cost of publishing. It was not something I'd done before, or would do again, but I wanted it to be circulated, and am glad Jennifer agreed to its importance, hosting the launch with Alex as guest of honour. He died after an illness two years later, but at least his exploits during the war were on record under a new title, *Dragons In The Forest*. I had hoped there might be a French translation, but unfortunately this was not followed up, and because of its neglect now seems unlikely.

The third and final book she published was *The Last Double Sunrise*, launched at the site of a prisoner of war camp in Cowra, adjacent to where I'd trained as an army recruit. Basically, it is the story of an Italian boy who becomes a skilled artist. His talent divides the family; encouraged by his mother, violently opposed by his father, he wins a coveted art scholarship at the famous gallery, the Villa Medici in Rome. The promising career is halted when war breaks out. Forced into the army, he is captured, sent to Britain as a POW, then transferred to that same Cowra camp in Australia.

If I may quote from a review by novelist Dorothy Johnston:

> *His trials and dangers, his hopes and feelings and ambitions are a joy to read. The story of Italian prisoners of war, first in England, then Australia, is fascinating in itself, and told with verve and compassion.* The Last Double Sunrise *confirms Peter Yeldham's reputation as an outstanding writer of historical fiction.*

Thank you Dorothy. It was nice to go out on such an upbeat note!

I finished writing that book just weeks before my 90th birthday. There was an inevitable party which I tried to avoid, but my daughter would not be swayed, declaring it was all arranged. You have to celebrate reaching that impressive number, she told me. So friends and cousins assembled at her house, to see if I still had sufficient breathe to blow out the candles. Mercifully there were just nine candles, not 90.

My grand-daughters cleverly used some old photos to create an entertaining tape that took us back 89 years, to when I was a smiling bundle in a pram. They'd combined other snapshots that I didn't know existed, some with my brothers, lots with Marge and our growing children, a few of my mother that escaped the Elf's malicious act, as well as pictures posed long after those times, outside the Wig and Pen Club in London's Fleet Street. It was a lovely afternoon. More than that, it was a special family day; the warmth and kindness was unforgettable, but I had the usual problem of trying to hear all that was being said.

I probably inherited deafness from my father, and by the late sixties had to use a hearing aid. Some people can cope with it, but despite the aids I could never hear in large gatherings, which seriously restricts a social life. When I moved back to Sydney there were a growing number of dinner parties, Writers Guild and industry events as well as attending plays and movies. Gradually I had to give up most of it. At cinemas the screen dialogue became difficult to hear. In restaurants the clatter of cutlery drowned conversation. There was a sanctuary in Cremorne where I often had lunches with close mate Tom Hegarty. Two at a table was no problem, but in time our meetings attracted four or five other writer friends. Released from their keyboards, the pastime of most writers is an exchange of gossip, so I sat through long lunches trying to hear the conversations and follow enough words to give the impression I was taking part. Eventually, and very reluctantly, I had to give up these luncheons, just as I had to decline invitations from the industry to attend award nights.

Those who are fortunate not to suffer from this, have no idea how much it inhibits camaraderie and, without exaggeration, shuts off contact with much of the ordinary world. After a few refusals and apologies, the invitations stop coming. I still find conversation comfortable between two people, because of my hearing aid. A third person makes it slightly more difficult. Fast talkers and soft voices make it impossible. It's why so many convivial gatherings are now avoided, because I can no longer participate or enjoy them.

It all comes with escalating age, which is not a period I recommend. My friend and first agent Beryl Vertue says she's not in favour of it either. I have a particular dislike for a popular television event which announces its presences by a caption: STAY YOUNGER **LONGER.**

"TOO LATE, MATE" was my shouted reply at the screen the first time. And the other times it appears, of course. I've become a shouter at screens, ever since no longer writing till midnight, then reluctantly leaving a note for myself about the first line that will help me begin the next morning. These days I'm more likely to spend the time wondering if any of the things I began and then abandoned on cupboard shelves in my study could surprise me. There's a lot of discarded work in there, most of it half finished, perhaps even a good idea lurking in a corner, or on a top shelf. There are two musicals that never managed to reach the stage. The first one, long ago in England was a riotous romp in 17th century London called *Tiddy Dol*, with music by Richard Hill. I think we were unlucky, or chose the wrong producer, because many years ago it nearly got there. Richard and I spent a morning with some West End luminary whose name has escaped me, mainly over who should play the lead. We could not find a star that pleased him, including Keith Michel. We tried to remind him that Keith had played the lead in three very successful musicals, *Robert and Elisabeth*, *Irma La Douce* and *Man of La Mancha*. This West End person told us that in his opinion Keith was not really a star, so we left after telling him in our opinion he was certainly not a producer. It travels with me, that manuscript, if only to remind me we should've persevered, the music and lyrics were worth it.

Another musical: *James and Maggie* was about the life and loves of James Cassius Williamson with music by David Reeves. We joined a weekend at St Kilda with others trying out songs from shows they'd put together. It was a charming interlude, but nobody's work won any prizes, or received an invitation to open in Melbourne.

Apart from musical detours there are the remnants of tv scripts, the start of a thriller called *Knife Edge*, and the first hundred pages of a book about a young Englishman, falsely accused of theft and on the run, who ends up at the Eureka stockade. I have a feeling they'll all remain there on their shelves, and will probably end up as a sizeable contribution at the local tip.

Meanwhile old age brings fond memories of places and people, and revives the pleasure I found in travel. Like many of our era we were late starters. Our generation belonged to an era when it was difficult, and at times impossible to go overseas. Growing up in wartime we couldn't leave the country, and when peace came, most of us could not afford to travel. The crowded military ship to Japan was an adventure to me. The next time I went anywhere was to England on the *Fairsea*, eight years later.

It seems extraordinary in this day and age, to admit I never flew in a plane until I was almost thirty, a flight that was just a channel hop from London to Paris. We certainly made up for it afterwards. Because of the Writers Guild agreement with film producers there were lots of first class flights to interesting places, but I recall more fondly the family journeys. Each summer we went south to the sunshine of Portugal, Greece, Italy, Spain or Majorca, while every winter Marge took Lyn and Perry skiing in Austria or Switzerland. I stuck to the summer holidays after my only winter venture, where I kept trying to follow my children down the slopes, and ending on my arse in the snow.

On one of those summer holidays we drove across Europe, through what was then Tito's Yugoslavia, to reach Athens, spending two months there with Greek friends. Albufeira in Portugal was another favourite place where we had holidays. It was where we met Canadian writer, Donald McKenzie. When Donald knew us better the next time we went there, he entrusted Marge and me with his secret past. After a long night with what used to be called 'a few grogs' he told us of his life as a jewel thief in Quebec and London, where he pulled off some celebrated robberies. After two arrests, knowing he'd face a long sentence if there was a third, he reformed, moved to Portugal, married a charming redhead, and wrote an autobiography called *Gentleman of Crime*. He followed it with several more books, and by the time we met he was a successful writer of thrillers. He often stayed with us in London, and one night was alone when our neighbours, Peter and Betty Lambda, came seeking help, having locked themselves out of their flat. As he didn't know them, Donald was in a quandary, and told us about it when we came home.

"I could have busted the lock in ten seconds," he said, "but thought it tactful to call a police locksmith. Your neighbours might not welcome a house-breaker next door."

Donald was a great character, one of many we met in the nineteen sixties and early seventies, when Albufeira was a charming town. *A secret gem* the British newspapers called it, but after that it was neither secret, nor a gem. Developers moved in, and on our last visit the landscape had changed. Olive groves and vineyards had been replaced by apartment blocks. Today it is apparently full of gated communities, where visitors rarely mix with locals, or take leisurely strolls through the lanes to the mixed markets we knew, for the town is now mostly shopping malls and private clubs.

I often think of other lovely places, and wonder if the travel supplements have turned those hideaways into honeypots. *Sant Antoni*, our Spanish house on the beach, now consists of affluent villas. I learned this at the dentist's, thumbing through a magazine in his waiting room. But for the name I would not have known the place. The centre page revealed a glitzy resort, with houses for sale and yacht marinas for hire. No longer a quiet beach with rentals at a quid a week!

I wonder if the magical island of Rhodes has been spoiled. Vincent Ball went on a cruise of the Greek Islands, and said it was bedlam; tourist ships all landing their passengers at the same time, with the result that its historic charm was swamped by sightseers. We were there one quiet Easter, a school holiday with Perry. We hired a car to drive to the beach at Lindos, stopping at a roadside café for coffee.

It was soon after Carl Foreman had written and produced *The Guns of Navarone,* filmed on the island. The café owner had been an extra in the movie, and spoke fondly of Carl. When he learned we were friends and both were on the council of the Writers Guild, he declared our coffee was free. We protested, he insisted. A friend of Carl, who'd brought such prosperity to the island, was logically *his* friend. It's the Greek way.

We had to pass his café whenever we went for a swim on that holiday, and though we tried, we were never allowed to pay. His children played with our son, and in the way of kids who don't speak the same language, they understood each other perfectly. It was a charming friendly place. I can only hope the cruise ships haven't spoilt it.

In these days overseas trips are rare. I'm not fond of travelling alone, so it was a pleasure when Lyn and I had six weeks in London. She met up with her school friends, while I spent time with Janet Croyston, now living permantly there, and an old friend Chris Penfold who edits the long-running *Midsomer Murders*. We also had dinner with Beryl whose marvellous career, a successful producer with a stream of films and TV series, has earned her an OBE. While we were in the UK, Lyn and I had an afternoon with the current owners of Ashtead. It looked as lovely as ever. A truly magic house with ten acres surrounded by bush tranquillity, a mere half hour from London.

Should we have stayed there? I did wonder about it that sleepless night.

It was only my second visit to England in five years. Too many friends were missing, Donald Churchill and his wife Pauline are the main loss. They stayed with us in Sydney, and we stayed with them whenever we were in London, after selling our house on Kingston Hill. So many more who were part of our life there have passed on: Lord Ted Willis, to give him his full title, who persuaded me to write my first TV play. Among others, neighbours Peter and Betty Lambda, Bob Stewart, Tony Kearey, and of course Spike Milligan. Marge typed his scripts. I think this was her favourite Spike line:

BLOODNOK: Now Neddie, pull up a chair and sit down.
SEAGOON: I'd rather stand, if you don't mind.
BOODNOK: Well, in that case pull up a floor.

Whenever Spike came back from visiting his parents in Woy Woy, he'd ring us to say he had a couple of decent bottles of Aussie red awaiting our arrival. He could also enjoy embarrassing people. I once told him I was going to see a play he'd written and was also acting in. In the middle of a scene he suddenly announced to the audience "There is an Australian present in the fourth row. Kindly stand up, Australian, and be identified."

I stood, because I knew he'd keep on with it until I did.

"So, friend from Down Under, what's your opinion of England?"

Luckily by this time I'd thought of a reply.

"Well I came for two years and I'm still here after nearly ten. I must like it."

"You're almost one of us," he said, and went on with the play.

It was typical Spike. If his children took long showers and used up the hot water, he complained by sending a telegram to his wife, who was downstairs. He could not resist passing an empty funeral parlour, where he'd lie on the counter and bellow "SHOP". He enjoyed being bizarre, was often moody, but in my opinion deserved to be considered a genius. *The Goon Show* was unique. With it he changed comedy forever.

Lost friends in Australia are also too many to list, but the best and brightest are a fond memory. John McCallum and Googie Withers not only lent us their house, they were great companions. So were Morris and Joy West who came for weekends, and we all met on first nights at Marian Street Theatre, until it shut its doors, one more Sydney theatre lost through lack of support. Another close friend was John Croyston, a neighbour in both Cremorne and the Central Coast. Ray Barrett and I met back in the radio days. He was born the same year as me, seven days apart, and was fond of reminding me that I was a week older. When he arrived in England, he rang to tell me his first role was a script I wrote for Associated-Rediffusion. Over the years he was in many of my plays and series, especially when we both returned home. He starred in *Run From The Morning* and *Golden Soak*, played Bligh in *Timeless Land,* and the journalist in *Sporting Chance.*

About ten years ago I wrote an earlier private memoir with more emphasis on the family. That was when our seven grandchildren were growing up fast. I still remember them as a bunch of kids before they became adults, and recall the Christmas celebrations we enjoyed at Yarramalong. The house was always full at that time, and one year we had such an excess that we hired a caravan. There was a rush to claim the bunks. Anyone could sleep in a bed, but only the swift could claim a place in the van. They were memorable, those Christmas days with competitive games of cricket and croquet, and in the evenings even more competitive scrabble. My wife and grandson Pete were the stars of scrabble. The author mostly came a distant last.

The family tree has certainly grown. From seven grandchildren, at the last count, things have changed. My entry in *Who's Who* means I get a phone call before each time they publish, asking if there is a new book, or a change in my family. The most recent time, my caller asked if there was any change in the family list.

"You have three great-grandchildren," she said, quoting the list of a previous edition three years earlier.

"Slight change," I said. "I now have ten great-grandchildren."

The caller was suitably impressed.

While I can no longer face the tyranny of distance, the grandkids are all frequent fliers. Lyn's daughter Olivia was an early traveller to America, going to university there, then working in Indonesia, living in London after her marriage, and since then in Kenya. Phil and his wife Sara travel to her former home in Thailand, while Robert and his family now live in Canada. With two families of her grandchildren overseas, Lyn is a busy traveller.

Perry took his family to America and England long before they could go alone. He always says he saw so much of the world with us when he was growing up, he wanted his children to have the same experience. He's managed it; they had Christmas twice in England and once in America. Their son Pete's final university semester was at Nijmegen University in Holland, and their daughters Emily, Lydia and Bronwyn all spent their gap years working in Europe.

Emily now married, spent two years as a teacher in London, after which she and her husband, Robert, flew home with numerous stopovers, including Germany and Budapest, then Japan and Vietnam. Somewhere along the way they also found time to ski in the Pyrenees. Frequent fliers indeed. I envy them being able to travel so much, but glad they can do it. Our generation never experienced gap years, or trips to see the rest of the planet. It's a different sort of world now, and despite faults, or occasional horror headlines, I think it's a better one.

Which prompts the question, is Australia now a better country? Was it better in the post-war fifties, when we freely opened our borders to others, but callously branded them with names like wogs and dagoes? Despite that crude unfriendly reception many migrants proved to be high achievers, changing the way we live in this country, and improving it.

Australia was once a ferociously xenophobic place. Parts of it still are. In the early half of last century, it may not be widely known, but a prestigious publication like *The Bulletin*, declared on its masthead the words *A country for the white man*. It seems incredible that it went unchallenged for a great many years, and fortunately it is unlikely to be repeated, although who could count on it? The undercurrents of racial hatred are still there. Recently a senator stood in parliament and advocated that people "have a right to be bigots". An extraordinary statement. He now represents us in London, so I hope he devotes more care to what he says there or anywhere else. We still have politicians who would agree with *The Bulletin's* banner, like the woman who leads her own party of misfits, or the Liberal Party minister who walked out of parliament, rather than stay to hear Prime Minister Rudd's apology for past treatment of Indigenous children snatched from their homes and parents.

Multiculturalism has its critics, but I hope and believe acceptance is on the rise. I want to believe there is a growing decency amongst the young of this country, that will endure as the old and narrow-minded xenophobes leave the stage. In hopeful mood, I can only compare the Australia of today with the staid environment of my youth, when the censorship of anything radical was paramount, and its stultifying atmosphere of conformity sent many of us abroad in search of somewhere more tolerant. It was an enriching experience, that twenty years overseas. For the first time in our lives we were able to travel widely to other countries, freed from the restraints and limitations imposed on us in our homeland.

*****

PART TWELVE: INTERVIEWS AND AFTERTHOUGHTS

This begins with Susan Lever, author, critic and General Editor of Cambria Press who has twice interviewed me, as well as written an analysis of my play for the BBC, *Reunion Day: An Anzac Day Play on British Television* in the *Journal of the Association for the Study of Australian Literature*. Susan has interviewed and written about almost every screenwriter who has contributed to Australian television, in a major opus to be published soon.

We first met when she came to Yarramalong in 1998, after I'd recently finished writing *The Currency Lads*. We began with the biographical details and early days, that led to my father's dismay at my choice of a career.

"What prompted you to be a writer?" was Susan's first question.

I think I said Hemingway was something to do with it, as were a few Australian writers whom I read widely. But I think it was also fuelled by the fact my family was so much against it. We covered the psychiatrist visit, and the time when people knew little about radio writers, many of them prepared to believe actors made up the words. This belief was happily endorsed by some actors.

We also discussed the battle that writers had in those days when the low fees made us work non-stop, and how quantity, not quality, became the considered measure of success. After her questions and my answers regarding the years spent in London, a lot of it was devoted to work since my return, such as the first two miniseries, *Run From The Morning* that I'd written mostly in England, and *Ride On Stranger*, an adaptation of a book by Kylie Tennant, who became a friend. I'd enjoyed writing both. *Ride on* in particular was an absolute joy, because Liddy Clark was so good in it. She and Noni Hazlehurst were ideal casting, heading a fine group of actors. They were about the same age and great fun: I remember travelling by train with the pair of them, trying to conceal the fact it was my fiftieth birthday, when they suddenly opened a parcel and presented me with a cake, then sang a loud chorus of Happy Birthday.

In Susan's first interview she concentrated on the television I'd been writing in the past twenty years, then spoke of the book I'd just written, the *Currency Lads*. I dwelt on the large amount of research I did, and how vital it became. Learning the truth about some historical characters was a bonus that brought an extra reality to the characters, and hence to the story. William Charles Wentworth and the corrupt Benjamin Boyd were among those who came alive, Wentworth an acquisitive if relatively decent man, Boyd quite the opposite, with an arrogant disregard for the Pacific Islanders he imported to work on his land and mistreated. When his bank and other ventures failed he fled from the exposure, and was believed to have been killed in the Solomon Islands.

I was assisted, and gave credit to a fascinating book of paintings by Susanna Evans, *Historic Sydney as seen by its Early*

Artists. It provided me with several previously unknown people at that time, wonderful characters not in the history books, as they had been painted in the streets of early Sydney. One particular find for me was Samuel Lyon, a cheerful East Ender who ran an auction house. There was just one photo of him, but he became a popular figure in my story. I've always found research essential, and it has often been an asset in other novels, but never before as important as it was in this book.

Ten years later, in 2008, the Writers Guild invited me to be interviewed on film, and Susan again asked the questions. We covered the start when I'd turned seventeen, trying to write short stories that would appeal to afternoon newspapers; then the initial years of radio where, like most tyros, I was tested on routine quarter-hour scripts, such as *Doctor Mac*. After that the eighteen months in Japan, and the years in an increasingly busy world of radio, dreaming some impossible dreams, such as someday being able to write screenplays for films.

Then our move to Britain: television plays for the BBC and Plays of the Week, as well as scripts for many of the series there. The finest series by far was *Probation Officer*, the best I ever worked on. After that films followed by a change to stage plays, and writing two for the stage in collaboration with close friend Donald Churchill. I told Susan how much I enjoyed touring to test each play before audiences in towns all over England, aiming for a destination desired by all playwrights, a season in London's West End. Three of my plays did reach there, going on to productions overseas.

It was a very pleasant interview, hardly noticing time pass as we covered the return to Australia, and how stage plays became a sacrifice. I found touring was rare, and most theatrical managements avoided it because of costs and the lack of enough suitable theatres. I wrote just one stage play, *Split Down The Middle*, that was staged at the Marian Street Theatre, and had seasons in New Zealand and Perth. Another, called *Once A Tiger*, had a reading with actors, and was produced overseas. The only other theatrical event was when David Reeves asked me to rewrite scenes for his musical *Seven Little Australians*. We worked with the cast in Melbourne before we moved to the Comedy Theatre for dress rehearsals, then a week of previews with audiences. These were intense with conferences afterwards sometimes over midnight meals; it was familiar territory and tremendously enjoyable. The show was a success in Melbourne, packing the Comedy Theatre. When Michel Noll came from Paris to Australia and wanted to see the musical, I managed to get him the last seat at a mid-week matinee.

If stage plays no longer played a part in my life, Susan's questions revealed television certainly did. From my arrival home, the following fifteen years included a succession of mini-series. Nineteen of them during that time, all of the final drafts of these scripts and details of their productions are now with the National Film and Sound Archive.

The first ones were for the ABC, produced at the Forest Studios by Ray Alchin. After being back a few years, this extended to work for Channels Nine and Ten. I found them more difficult, because their drama departments had an abundance of experts, who were called script or story editors.

In all our work for the ABC and then for Resolution Films, Ray and I never had a script editor. If either of us had a problem with the script, we found it easy to talk and find a solution. We combined on ten miniseries, four telefilms and the episodes of *Sporting Chance*. All of these were a close collaboration without the outside help of editors or executive producers.

The interview filmed by Foxtel, is now stored with those of other writers in the archives. To be selected was an honour, and I place it with another tribute, being given the Richard Lane Award in 2001 for services to the Guild. For me it had a particular importance, as Richard Lane was always a friend, from my start at sixteen when he taught me so much about radio writing, until his death in 2008.

At the end of this interview I told Susan I was close to finishing my novel *A Distant Shore*, but not yet certain how it would end. I explained it was the way I worked, and had always done so. Uncertainty and unexpected events are what I find exciting, and this is why I resist plotting the fixed outline of a story ahead of time. In hindsight it was like a motto, and should have been one. Perhaps just a simple slogan would cover it: If writing stops being exciting, that's when I stop writing.

Over the years there were many Q&A sessions. The most memorable was the night at the National Film and Sound Archive with Meg Labrum. There were other notable nights, one in the Barossa Valley, as a guest of Mrs Lehmann at her vineyard. It was an open air dinner for several hundred people, organised by the Barossa library. A lot of very good wine flowed, and the questions and answers lasted long into the night. These sort of evenings were far more relaxed than the widely publicised and larger events like writers festivals and conventions.

There were also many interviews by email, just a few of the questions listed here.

> *From Nicole Alexander: What are the main differences between writing a novel and a film script. And which do you prefer?*
> I prefer novels. Films begin with a commission to write a screenplay. Novels begin with my own ideas, and stay with me until the book is finished.

> *From Tim Kroenert – of theWriters Guild. What are the key differences between plays and books?*
> Books need far more description. To take a simple example. In plays a character can be described as 'in her forties,

attractive' which is all a director needs for casting, but in a novel this is inadequate. Editors want full descriptions; height, style, hair colour, the clothes they wear. With my first books I was continually being asked for much more personal detail of each character. I'd learned the habits of not describing enough detail through years of writing television and films.

Another question Tim posed was the subject of 'big print', a term for stage directions.
Too much big print is tedious. Directors get fed up with scripts where the big print suggests every move. A director friend of mine went berserk when given exact instructions on a script, and even worse, told why he should completely follow the given instructions. Shakespeare gave no directions, apart from telling actors when to enter or leave the stage.

In 2005 there was an interview with Memorable TV, covering the years from being a messenger boy trying to be a radio writer. It was an intense interview, that seemed to know all the television I'd written in Britain and Australia, but also every screenplay, the stage plays and the novels since then. In conclusion it asked me what domain I'd enjoyed most?
Novels was the easy answer, but it made me realise all of them had attractions. Theatre was wonderful in England. So was much of the television there that led me to Films. TV in Australia was also exciting in the nineteen seventies and eighties, until it became stifled with treatments. Today I'm glad to be no longer writing for television. It seems to be weighed down with one of my least favourite sights With my last TV show the executive producers were listed on succeeding screens; there were too many names to fit on only one.

What are you most proud of writing was Memorable TV's last question.
It's a brute of a question. I selected *Captain James Cook*, although I hated the title. I could as easily pick one of the books. There's a great deal I like about *The Currency Lads* and *Against The Tide*. Both were published with hardly an editorial pencil making a change. Or there's my English tv play *Stella*. It was superbly directed, and highly praised.

Over the years there have been interviews with newspapers and radio. I haven't kept any, apart from this one from the Australian *Times*.

Q: What do you most enjoy about being a freelance novelist?
A: Being able to write what I wish, and never be told what to write. And a lifetime of never having to wear a collar or tie.

This began with an empty page and is close to a final one. To my surprise in 1991, I received an Order of Australia Medal and later a Centenary medal *for services to the Arts as a screenwriter.* That meant a great deal. Growing up in an environment where we unknowingly jettisoned world rights for radio scripts, I became an advocate for the protection of royalties and residuals. It was an injustice our radio shows were sold to so many countries without payment. The early days of television were the same: radio and television were thriving industries, but the only ones who thrived were the owners of the networks. Not the writers, until we formed groups to combat this injustice. I became a member of the British Writers Guild when Ted Willis restructured it in 1960, serving on its executive committee for eight years. Returning home, I spent two terms on the Australian council, and was Vice President to David Williamson. This was rewarded by a singular accolade, the honorary membership of both Guilds.

In those years our council contained many busy writers who gave up their time, like Roger Simpson, John Dingwall, Tony Morphett, Tom Hegarty, Margaret Kelly, Geoffrey Atherden, Moya Wood, Ted Roberts and Cliff Green. We were fortunate to have Angela Wales as Executive Officer. In my opinion Angela transformed the Australian Guild from the day she took over. That it now occupies a position of influence is largely due to her.

I did join the Society of Authors, but felt no bond there. It was strange, being so much involved in both screen guilds, but felt the ASA was always remote, like a select club where no-one attempted to make contact. I barely knew anyone there. I did know Tom Kenealley when we both lived in Avalon, but lost touch with him when we moved from there. The only exception was Jon Cleary. We were long time friends, often met, or exchanged letters, and I include his last one here, for it is so characteristic of him. Letters from real friends are like cheerful conversation, and this remains for me like a final chat with Jon.

Dear Peter,
I was really bucked to get your letter and the comments on "Morning's Gone". I'm still working on my 1948 'writer, and the bloody thing is unreliable in its old age. My grandkids tell me I'm the same way ... I've just published my last book. I don't have the stamina any more, and it's better to go out while some of the reviews are still good. I saw a good review for your last book and hope the sales warrant the time you spent on it. But tastes are changing, and the book trade ain't what it was when I came into it those years ago. Publishers aren't the same—now the game is run by conglomerates, interested only in the bottom line, not the words. I hope your health is still good. I'm shaky in the legs, but that's to be expected. My doc told me I have a

50 year-old-head, but below the neck I'm coming up to 90. I notice it –I pass a pretty girl, the head turns, but the body keeps going straight ahead.
Take care. And keep writing. Jon

It was typical Jon. I enjoyed the fact he was bashing away on a sixty year old typewriter. There were times when I wished I could discard the computer and do the same.

I'd discussed most things with Jon, but not my feelings about the Society of Authors. It was strange not to feel a rapport, because the most satisfying period of my working life has been the time devoted to novels.

I think the satisfaction has come from the freedom of being able to tell a story that starts and grows in my mind. No-one, apart from Marge, shared any details of most books until they went to a publisher, the exemption being Perry and Mary Anne, and those with us in France before I started *Barbed Wire and Roses*.

I've never had, or wanted a government grant, let alone an advance before writing novels. It's a different ball game with films or television. I'm referring to books here, and there's been a simple reason why I feel this way. It means there is no-one with fixed ideas awaiting the outcome, no instructions or formula to be followed; it allows total freedom to choose my own subject and create my own characters. The publisher and editor have their turn later, but I always want to start with no rules or restraints, no directives, and when it happened to be films or television, then no producer, or Head of Drama trying to put their stamp on it. I like to start with a character and a concept, and never be obliged to follow a strict outline. I enjoy writing when I'm able to work out the story as I go, and while it's been harder after Marge died, it's also been a lifesaver in the solitary years since then. I have just one regret, that I didn't begin writing novels much earlier.

There have been ups and downs in a very long career. A lucky bugger, some have said, being in England during the best years for television in the nineteen sixties. But not always fortuitous when Sydney Box's dazzling offer vanished. Or the loss of my friend, Ray Alchin, and the outstanding film of early Sydney we could have made together.

I have indeed been lucky, able to earn a living from something I enjoy so much, and fortunate to have two children whom I love. Most of all fortune favoured me in a private and particular way. After an unhappy family existence in the early years, I found someone special to share the future with, and she enriched my life.

© Peter Yeldham 2019.

PART THIRTEEN: EMAILS, DIARIES, LETTERS AND SELECTED WORKS

The following pages contain letters from publishers, from the ABC, from a few readers, and a diary I kept of the play *Birds On The Wing*, from the evening of the first idea to all that happened afterwards.

A FEW EMAILS

I was agreeably surprised at the flood of emails that came with my novels set in period Australia. It began with *A Bitter Harvest*, continued with *The Currency Lads* and really took off with *Barbed Wire and Roses*. I'd filled a post-office box, but had to get another for *Barbed Wire*, then yet another for *A Distant Shore* and *Glory Girl*. It was interesting and inspiring, the enthusiasm for *A Distant Shore* with its compassion for asylum seekers.

As well as local emails, many came from Canada, New Zealand and South Africa. Felicity Giles in Cape Town wished her blind husband could share my books with her. Putting her in touch with Audio Publishing's Pauline Meaney, she obtained discs and wrote to say how they both enjoyed being able to discuss each book.

Another special reader was Val Bradshaw from Townsville who shares my feeling for asylum seekers. She found me through the internet and wrote to say she'd just finished listening to *A Distant Shore*. Val is a remarkable woman, she read and commented on several of my books, her letters so fluent and interesting that I always looked forward to them. She lost her sight in middle age, but not her bright attitude to life.

Message from Val Bradshaw:
Hello Peter, I have just finished listening to your book The Distant Shore, *what a wonderful book you write with so much compassion, one could almost believe that the story was personal and the story really touched my heart, I too would be out there fighting for these very unfortunate people were I younger and had my sight.*

From Sue Neilson (September 2009):
I am just writing to say how much I am enjoying your books. My first of your novels was Barbed Wire and Roses *and it just hooked me in!! The character of Stephen suffered so much in*

WW1 and I felt for him incredibly. Since then I have read The Murrumbidgee Kid, Against the Tide *and* A Distant Shore *and I look forward to the others. I find you have a marvellous way of bringing the characters to life and giving the reader an insight into how people think and react the way they do. Once I start reading your books there is no stopping me until I have finished (much to my family's chagrin at times!!) As I said I look forward to purchasing the next few books and hope to hear of a new one soon. Thank you so much for sharing your stories with us.*

From Sheila Dowrick (November 2009):
I've just finished reading your book A Distant Shore—*what a fabulous read!!!!*
Funnily enough half way through reading the book, I received one of those emails, you know the kind "This is our country, and if these people can't or won't change their ideas, they should go home". Although I agreed basically with what the email said, before forwarding it on to my many cyber friends I added an addendum, to the effect that all boat people, etc, should at least be treated AS HUMAN BEINGS, and given a chance. If they blew that chance, then by all means throw the book at them (and I didn't mean your book !!!!).
Thank you for making me think about this—I've never been anti-muslim, or anti anything else to be honest, but sometimes what comes out of my mouth doesn't reflect what is in my heart—I guess you made me think before opening said mouth.

From Amanda Fonti (December 2009):
Hi, I received your book A Distant Shore *as a Christmas present this year. It was the best book I have read. I could not put the book down.*
I just wanted to say thank you for a wonderful book. Kind regards.

Part Thirteen: Emails, Diaries, Letters and Selected Works

From Jackie McDonald (September 2010):
Dear Peter Yeldham, greetings from New Zealand. Despite being an avid reader of many, many years, this is the very first time I have ever written to an author—I do hope you don't mind.
I have just read your Barbed Wire and Roses *and I was so moved by the story that reduced me to tears. A wonderful, wonderful, book and one that I will never forget. It is quite interesting, having been educated in the UK—the British Empire and Rule Britannia and all that, that when one goes to live in another country and immerses themselves in the culture of that adopted country how views change. I know that the WW1 was a shambles, but I did not know just how shameful the British administration was, and I certainly did not know that the French shot their own.*
I have read several other of your books, have recommended them highly to all my friends.
Thank you SO much for such a rewarding and thought-provoking book—I look forward to the next one. Kindest regards.

From Mary Stewart (December 2010):
Dear Peter, I've had the pleasure of enjoying another two of your amazing stories. As yet I've not read Against the Tide *but thank you for suggesting it. I did read* A Distant Shore *and I got a flavour of your passion for immigration. In my experience and discovery of Australia I've only known of those first immigrants who came here as prisoners and not of all those others who came since and didn't experience a welcoming country from those who call themselves immigrants but are all actual visitors to a country that doesn't belong to anyone except Aboriginals.*
I loved A Distant Shore, *I enjoyed your character Kate and her compassion. I often hear about 'boat people' and I must admit I have never given them any of my consideration. I want*

to thank you for Kate, what I love about the books I so enjoy that you write is that they give me more than a story. I now have a new interest in anyone from any situation who would love to consider moving to Australia and that in this day and age that they have to endure Detention Centres really is quite unbelievable.

Now I must admit to a struggle. I have also read A Bitter Harvest. *Wow, that for me was a truly amazing story. I loved every single word on every page. The period, the history, the characters. You took me on an amazing journey that I would be hard pushed now to pick between this book and my first true love of* Barbed Wire and Roses.

I loved Sydney at that time, the Barossa valley, travelling through Melbourne, the establishment of Federation. My most memorable part is the understanding of Canberra. To anyone you ask outside of Australian most will answer that Sydney is our Capital City. The history and stories you have given behind the politics of the time have embedded within me that I will forever remember that Canberra also means womens' breasts and I also know why the state was formed for federation.

From Barbara Humphrey (August 2017):
Dear Peter, Just a little note to say thank you for your extraordinary novel A Bitter Harvest. *The saga of the Patterson and Muller families was deeply absorbing. I have experienced every emotion possible while reading of their loves and losses.*
Most of all thank you for opening my eyes to the appalling injustice suffered by those poor people in Hahndorf and the Barossa valley.
Works such as this are so important when so much of our Australian history is hidden. Cheers.

*****

THE DIARY OF A PLAY

1967
September

The winter was always my favourite time for writing in England, and after spending half a year writing a film for an American company, the Mirisch Bros, which despite their promises of a serious World War Two epic had turned out to be a fairly routine story and a disappointing chore, I felt I had to take a step into the unknown and write a stage play. I was soon to be forty years old, and had never written one.

The idea had been simmering in my mind because of the mink coat; a light comedy about two girls, expert confidence tricksters who go around the world fleecing gullible men who want to get into their knickers. But in New York they meet Charlie Jackson, whom they trick out of his dollars, but who follows them to Paris and turns out to be a bigger crook than they are. The three form a team, and Charlie eventually sleeps with both girls and they all double-cross each other, which is what they like doing best.

Problem was, the play had to keep moving from city to city: New York to Paris, London, Istanbul, Tokyo. It was while staying in the Hilton in Athens that Marjorie and I realised all Hilton hotel rooms look the same. Change a picture on the wall and a backdrop view, and you can be anywhere. (This was later ascribed by one critic to a flash of genius by the stage designer.)

I called the play *Birds on the Wing* and in October of 1967 began work.

October/November/December, January (1968)

I suggested to Terry Nation, a friend who wrote *Dr Who* and invented the Daleks, that we should work together. We lasted only four days, most of it spent drinking coffee, then he got a lucrative assignment writing a TV series *The Persuaders* for Roger Moore and Tony Curtis. So I decided to do it alone, asking my agent to turn down all film and TV offers, not even tell me about them, and spent four months writing. I had help and encouragement from Marge, and from my friends Peter Lambda and Betty Paul who lived in the same block of flats in Old Brompton Road, London. There were the usual desperate days, when nothing would go right and it all seemed hopeless, and then the great days when twists and new ideas seem to flood in, and a final version was typed at the end of January, 1968.

February, 1968
I sent it off to my agent, and went back to writing for a living.

Beryl, my agent, liked it. The rest of the month was silence.

March
Michael Codron was interested in trying it out at Richmond. This was most exciting, because Codron was a top theatre management.

Richmond Theatre read and liked it. Two days later Richmond Theatre didn't like it.

April
Codron went off it.

April and May
My agent sent the play to Coventry (Theatre). Hugh Jenkins, who I'd worked with at Granada TV, now ran this theatre. He didn't like it.

She sent it to Guildford – who wouldn't be able to read it for some time.

She sent it to Peter Bridge Management who turned it down. My agent prevailed on Tom Earhardt who worked for Bridge to read it. Earhardt liked it, and it transpired Bridge had only read the first few pages. Tom persuaded Bridge to read the rest of it.

June
Two weeks later and Peter Bridge had now read it. Interested. My agent excited. Bridge – who I only knew by repute – would phone me over Bank holiday weekend.

We went off to our weekender in Kent. P Bridge didn't phone. Golf games were cancelled, invitations refused, while I waited by the phone. A Bank holiday weekend is a long time when the phone doesn't ring. We returned to London.

Bridge rang to say he'd lost my weekend number. We'd meet soon. He suggested June 4th.

June 4th.
We heard the terrible news that Robert Kennedy had been killed. We decided it was not a day to talk of such things as plays – and I went home feeling sickened that another Kennedy had been assassinated.

Late June, 1968
Nigel Patrick was sent the play, read it swiftly and was keen to direct. We met at Bridge's office, and discussed casting. The girls would be difficult to cast, he said. Nigel suggested he not only direct, but also play Charlie. Since he was a good actor and a drawcard it was warmly agreed by all, including me. After all—nearly six months had elapsed, and I wanted to see some action.

Late July
Peter Bridge went to Australia. Nigel went to the seaside with his family. Bridge was horrified on his return that we had not been busy rewriting. Nobody had suggested rewrites until now, but P Bridge said we must know it needed rewrites, and he was disappointed we hadn't done them.

Guildford theatre had now read it, and were keen to have it done there.

August 1968
More meetings. Script changes suggested. I rewrote. More difficulties about casting the right girls; this was the main topic of conversation. Nyree Dawn Porter said she couldn't play it. Pru Scales said no thanks. Anna Massey liked it, but really wanted to do a drama. Moira Lister said she was too old – which was true.

September
No progress. Nigel Patrick away directing another play. Peter Bridge becoming testy with his absence. He has an inspiration. Sends the play to Ian Carmichael, who reads it immediately and loves the role.

An immense fall-out with Nigel Patrick, who rang me to say Bridge had double-crossed him and was offering it to Carmichael. It was now a year since I sat down to start writing it, and I am caught in the awful dilemma of two people fighting over the role and both trying to enlist my support.

But Bridge is over the moon at getting Carmichael. Ian is now cast as Charlie. Nigel Patrick has departed vowing never to speak to us again, though he occasionally rings me to bitch on about Bridge. Guildford pressing for the play. Exciting, ain't it!

October
Finally met with Ian Carmichael, instead of just listening to him on the telephone. He is now besieged by other offers. He is unsure what to do. Some days of nail-biting and suspense.

Still October
Ian finally decides. He turns them all down, and will play the role of Charlie. Actor Colin Gordon agrees to direct the play.

November
Spent a few days in Switzerland with Jack Cardiff. Had to return to meet Ian, P Bridge and Colin Gordon on November 5th. (*Fireworks day*) We argue about the first scene, which Ian and Colin hate. I agree to rewrite it. Casting talk on who will play the girls gets nowhere.

November 9th
Delivered new first scene. Ian asked if he could be frank, and I said he could be anyone he liked, if he'd just make up his mind. What he meant was, he prefers the original first scene. Colin prefers the rewrite.

Nov 11th 1968
Armistice Day. We meet to try to sort things out. Bitter arguments

all day, with Colin Gordon and Ian in opposite corners, and me in the middle. P Bridge went tactfully out to lunch with his wife. Ends in compromise all round, but it is obvious Ian and Colin do not see eye to eye on anything.

Time running out for a January start. We agree to meet Thursday for a down to earth session, at which we will definitely cast the girls.

Nov 14th (Thursday)
Probably the most futile day of my life. We argue, toss names back and forth. Ian is adamant; he will not do this play without two stars. Nobody can agree on who are stars. Those we agree on are not available. Those eager and available are not stars. Peter Bridge negative and lacking enthusiasm. I can see him looking for escape hatches. He reveals he hates the title! The meeting breaks up gloomily.

Nov 22nd
My agent, Beryl and I meet with P Bridge to try to establish if he really wishes to proceed. He says he does – *even if he hates the title*. We want to try to retain Ian Carmichael, as he is a West End draw, but Bridge says he has lost confidence in Ian. He says Ian is a neurotic bastard.

He persuades me to go into an adjoining office, ring Nigel Patrick and ask him if he would re-join the play. Nigel is relaxed and pleasant to me, but says – no offence, old boy, but would I tell Peter Bridge to go and get fucked.

Same Day: later
We (Bridge, Beryl and I) decide to approach Patrick MacNee who finishes "The Avengers" soon. Through Terry Nation who is a friend of his I arrange to meet him.

Nov 23rd
Meet Pat MacNee and give him the script. He promises to read it swiftly and phone. P Bridge returns from Belfast, where he has a production, and writes to MacNee. But no word from MacNee that week.

Nov 29th

Charming letter received from Ian – loves the play, likes me, but it means goodbye. I ring him and we talk for ages. He is worried by the lack of any co-stars and Bridge's ebbing enthusiasm, and has opted to do a Keith Waterhouse and Willis Hall play instead. (But not yet signed!)

We have just gone back six months – and it is ten months since I finished the play. The whole situation is paralysing, and I am barely able to think of writing anything. Our remaining hope rests with 'The Avenger'.

December 4th 1968

Finally heard from Pat MacNee. Not directly, nor did he reply to Bridge's letter. He simply gave the play back to Terry Nation, and said he liked it, but his accountant had suggested he'd save tax if he worked abroad after "The Avengers". He's going to America – to Los Angeles, and may the rotten, discourteous bugger stay there!

Telephoned P Bridge with this news, and he said – "Oh dear, I'm so sorry for you." It seemed like a disclaimer – I think his thoughts and ideas are now elsewhere.

Dec 10th

Met with Beryl. Decided this cannot go on. Alistair Foot and Tony Marriot (co-writers who have put on several of their own plays, and are currently trying out a new one, called "No Sex Please, we're British" with Michael Crawford) would like to meet with me – no obligation on either side

Dec 11th

Meeting arranged with Foot and Marriot for next week. No word from Bridge for a week. No suggestions. No ideas. Nothing.

Dec 15th

Met with Foot and Tony Marriot. Encouraging meeting, but nothing conclusive. They did ask if I'd like to invest in their new play "No Sex, etc" as I invested £200 in their last production and lost the lot. I said no thanks, with a title like 'No Sex Please we're British", and unknown star like Michael Crawford, I didn't think it had a chance.

(Small addendum to this. Alistair Foot died just before the play opened in the West End. Tony Marriot became extremely rich. I met him years later, and he roared laughing while explaining my £200 would have become at least £8000. And this was only halfway through its 20 year run.)

Dec 17th

Beryl managed to call Peter Bridge, who has been evasive. He feels certain Ian is still interested. We will all make decisions about a Guildford try out and dates after the New Year. Last Christmas I was finishing the final scene before revising the play, convinced of fame and fortune by Easter!

1969

Jan 5th.

Peter Bridge says Ian Carmichael is no longer a neurotic bastard, nor has he signed to do Keith and Willis's play. He is still interested – provided we can get a new director.

Jan 11th 1969

John Neville approached to direct. Agrees! The following day I met him. I love John Neville. He's a fun person, and a great actor – and clearly most intelligent, *as he likes the play!* Suggests Zena Walker as one "bird".

Jan 16th

Zena Walker approached to play Samantha, but has agreed to do another play. Peter Bridge rushed a copy of the script to her. Zena enthusiastic. Ian Carmichael returns on Sunday. We wait with bated breath to see if he likes Zena Walker, and whether he considers her a "star".

Peter Bridge has decided to approach the Hilton hotel, since the play is set in its hotel rooms around the world, to see if they want to be involved. The Hilton read it and responded that guests never rob each other, and crooks do not stay at a Hilton. They threaten to sue if we dare to use their name! Not the cleverest move by P Bridge.

Jan 19th (Sunday)
Ian returns. Tells me on the phone he loves Zena Walker, and why didn't we think of her long ago.
Jan 20th
Meeting with P Bridge, John Neville and Ian. Very successful. Zena Walker has agreed to sign: everyone loves Zena, especially Ian. John Neville pleased, because he suggested her. Bridge has decided to tour it extensively prior to the West End and forget Guildford. Arguments about rehearsal times, dates of tour, etc., but at least we are talking. I go home so enthused I call friends for drinks. Marge and I mildly pissed.
Jan 21st
Contract arrives at my agents. Agreed and signed within hours. Beryl tells me Alistair Foot rang up definitely wanting the play – but it is no longer possible. Peter Bridge still hates the title "Birds on the Wing", and I have spent weeks submitting new ones – which everyone else hates.
Jan 27th
Mart Crowley, currently in London for his huge success "The Boys in the Band", was in Bridge's office. He saw a copy of my play, and said according to Peter's secretary: "Birds on the Wing – that's a good title." Collapse of stout party (P Bridge), and end of discussions on the title.

Angela Scoular, funny, kooky actress chosen as Liz, the other girl. Subject to contracts we now have our three leads. Other casting starts. Rehearsals to begin.
Feb 24th
What a lovely day. Rehearsals began on schedule at the Irish Club in Belgravia. Went well – except sometimes when Ian could not manage to do a piece of business, John Neville would do it to show him how – and was much better.
March 23rd Edinburgh
First night of the tour at The King's Theatre, Edinburgh. Great first night. Wonderful audience. The magic sound of a full house

laughing at lines I've written seems to be worth all the travail of the last year. This is a very friendly city where cab drivers wish you good luck for the first night. (They should say "break a leg", but who cares. London cabbies wouldn't bother to say a word.) John Neville, Marge and I have become great friends. We three stay up drinking after the first night until dawn.

The tour, 1969

The tour was 13 weeks, which is unusually long. In the middle, after five towns in England, there was a three week detour to Toronto. The cast and the set were flown to Canada, and we played in the O'Keefe Centre, which seated over a thousand people. It was full every night, and the Bridge Company reaped a bonanza. The playwright didn't do badly either! Peter Bridge did an amazing thing. Finding out it was our wedding anniversary, he flew Marge first class to Toronto. We had a great time in Canada, apart from the strange alcohol laws. John Neville, Marge and I went looking for a drink after sunset, and discovered it was almost impossible.

The size of the theatre was quite a contrast after the intimate Theatre Royal type playhouses we'd been in for the first five weeks. All the cast had their own dressing rooms and bathrooms, so it was a shock for the actors to return to England and our next tour date – in darkest Birmingham. Small shared dressing rooms, a cramped backstage, relentless rainy weather.

May 1969

The tour was coming to an end. Financially successful – big royalties for the writer and everyone else – but it was far too long. Seriously too long. Ian Carmichael is a nervous actor, who had failed in the West End last time out, starring in the musical "I do, I do". He now started to get nervous about "Birds on the Wing". Back in England he kept asking his mates to see the show, judge it, and give him notes. Anthony Sharp said it should be extensively rewritten and redirected, and suggested he should do it. Ian agreed. A writer declared it could be improved by his rewrite, and this arrival of Carmichael's friends continued. I told Bridge Ian's neurotic tactics were upsetting the cast, John Neville and me.

On May 10th this all came to a head. I told Tony Sharp to go to buggery, Ian told me and P Bridge he'd lost faith in the play, and John Neville said Ian was a neurotic git – and John was off to start his own theatre. Ian sent me a letter, an apologetic resignation. I was glad he's out because it became unbearable.. but thought it meant the death of the play.

May 25th
The tour mercifully over at last. Decision taken to recast the role of Charlie. Also find a new director and start again. I don't believe it. This is bullshit, paving an easy exit for Bridge Productions. One and a half years of my life seemed to have been wasted.

June
Nothing else happened. Not one of our most cheerful summers.

July 1969
Sudden change: news from P Bridge. Harvey Medlinsky, American director of several Neil Simon plays, agrees to direct "Birds on the Wing". He suggested Bruce Forsyth as Charlie, as he had directed him in Simon's "Little Me", and thought he was terrific. I didn't think he was terrific – but was now fairly desperate.

I even contemplated revisiting Nigel Patrick, but Bridge said Patrick was an untrustworthy bastard. We went though lists of 'West End stars'. The play was in danger of becoming a statistic. The investors were asked to keep their investment on hold, until decisions were made. It was summer time, and most people were on holiday. Usually, we went with the kids to Spain or Portugal, but I was too edgy to go anywhere that year.

July 25th 1969
Bruce liked the play. I met him and liked Bruce. Julia Lockwood and June Barry were cast to play Liz and Sam. Both lovely. Both stars.

August 1969
Rehearsals with the new cast and new director started.
September 1969
The tour opened at the Royal Court, Liverpool. It was a happy company; everyone liked Bruce. June and Julia were great in their roles. We had a wonderful first night. Laughs from the start. Roger Hancock came. He is Tony Hancock's brother, a much nicer man than Tony, and one of the best laughers in the business. His happy roars of laughter can get a whole audience going – and he did on our opening night. It went like a dream. At the party afterwards, someone said the fatal words … "it'll run for years in London". Someone else said the film rights were certain to be sold. George Abbott, American producer, was apparently keen to take it to Broadway.
Sept 29th
Coventry. Third week of the tour. After the wonder of Liverpool, no laughs in Coventry. We played in a barn of a theatre, a great orchestra pit between the stage and the audience which may partly explain why it played most of the week in dead silence. Abbott arrived for the Saturday night to see a woeful performance by a now puzzled and dispirited cast. No laughs. Afterwards he said to me: "You must be mad thinking I'd take that fucking thing to Broadway? " He went off in his hired limo, never to be seen again.
October 1969
The Royal Theatre, Newcastle. Back in an intimate theatre the play came to life again. The Piccadilly Theatre was available in London, and we began previews there on Oct 17th.
Oct 18th
My agent rang. Great excitement. Harry Saltzman was interested in the film rights. He'd talked to Michael Caine, who was coming to the Saturday matinee. Mike Caine was a hot star, after "Alfie" and other films.
October 20th
Word from Caine's agent that he liked it. Word from Harry

Saltzman he would probably acquire the film rights to star Caine. But he would first wait for the opening night to be sure. He said he trusted the opinions of critics more than the enthusiasm of actors...!!

October 23rd
1969

Opened at the Piccadilly Theatre in London. It was just two years since I was fumbling with the first act, but it felt like a great deal longer.

The first night was a full house, a good performance. The reviews were mixed. Some very good ones, but not enough to build a big advance with Christmas and the pantomimes coming. My agent rang Saltzman. He was busy buying Technicolour and would be in touch. Two weeks later she rang again. He didn't return her call.

November

The play was just making it. Weekends good, Mondays and Tuesdays were lousy. The Piccadilly gets no passing trade, tucked away in a back street, behind the Circus. Not like the Globe or the Lyric in Shaftesbury Ave.

My son and I went to see Chelsea play football. It was packed. I thought – *if only I could get a quarter of this crowd into that theatre we'd run for a year.*

December 1969

Costs were being trimmed to keep the show open. I took a royalty cut. The weeks before Christmas were dire. Peter Bridge said the fault was either Bruce or the title – or the play. He said "Virginia Woolf" played to packed houses at the Piccadilly. It was not a white Christmas, just a bleak one.

1970 February

Almost two years since I finished writing it, the play closed. It had run only four months in London. At the end I felt sad and exhausted. For a long time I could not go to the theatre, or write anything. Marge found a country house for sale that we both loved, and we bought it.

1970 April
We moved from London to "The Oaks", Ashtead Woods. Nine acres, just thirty minutes from the West End – but a comfortable distance from the Piccadilly Theatre.

The play had been acquired by a German *Verlag* – who translate and sell to the many theatres in the main cities of Europe. It was taken by two brothers who owned the *Komodie* Theatre in Berlin. I was too discouraged to go to the first night, although they invited me. I'd had a gutful of this play, and was busy renovating a house. It was much more fun than writing plays.

May 1970
I'd changed agents. Beryl became a producer, but remained a friend. My new agent, Harvey Unna, spoke German, and sent me translations of the reviews from the Berlin first night. They were astonishingly good. In fact, they were raves.

May-October, 1970
The play ran in Berlin for its contracted six months. It closed because the theatre had contracted to do "Sleuth", which had been a success in Britain and all over the world. For some obscure reason, "Sleuth" failed in Berlin. They still had the scenery for "Birds " – called *Auf und Davon* there because the title did not translate. The cast were available. So they put it on again.

And Afterwards –
It ran to packed houses for two years. I went to the first anniversary, and was treated like a prince. The two brothers who owned the theatre became friends. We sat and looked across the Berlin wall, where they were unable to go, but I was allowed to visit. Looking at the guns and snipers, I decided to stay in West Berlin with them.

The same cast did a long season in Munich, and an extensive tour in German and many European cities. They kept sending me postcards from wherever they were playing. It opened in

Paris and ran to full houses there for over a year. It was the top grossing play in Europe in the 1971-72 season. It's been running on and off ever since.

"Birds" was done in Holland, France, Italy, Belgium, Sweden, Switzerland, Denmark and about twenty other countries. In Australia it starred Ron Fraser, Carmen Duncan and Pamela Stephenson, but unfortunately played at a theatre restaurant in Macleay Street. When I came back to Australia, a well-known producer told me he'd tried to acquire it for a long season at the Royal Theatre, but Royce Foster had beaten him to the Aussie rights.

That's the story of this play: you win some, you lose some!

It never sold film rights. It never did play Broadway, but played in many other American cities.

It did sell as a six-part series to the BBC, starring Richard Briers.

In 1997 – when I wrote this diary (from notes kept in the past)—it was thirty years after the play. It has continued being produced until 2019, now fifty two years after the play was written.

That's why I kept this diary – so I can recall that traumatic two and a half years. I wish I'd been as lucky with all my stage plays but I'm not sure I could have stood the strain.

Peter Yeldham 2018

Poster for the production of Birds on the Wing *in Toronto, Canada.*

Piccadilly Theatre

PROPRIETORS: PICCADILLY THEATRE LTD.
MANAGING DIRECTOR AND LICENSEE: DONALD ALBERY

By arrangement with DONALD ALBERY

PETER BRIDGE

presents

BRUCE FORSYTH
JUNE BARRY

and

JULIA LOCKWOOD

in

BIRDS ON THE WING

A New Comedy

by

PETER YELDHAM

with

ERIC DODSON

DAVID TATE   JOSIE KIDD

CECIL CHENG   JOHN HART DYKE   ARNOLD LEE

Directed by
HARVEY MEDLINSKY

Designed by
HUTCHINSON SCOTT

Costumes by
TOM LINGWOOD

Lighting by
MICHAEL NORTHEN

Music composed by EWAN WILLIAMS

9

Programme credits for the London production of Birds on the Wing, *starring Bruce Forsyth.*

Poster for the German production of Birds on the Wing.

Statement of Significance

Cultural Gifts Program
Subdivision 30-A of the *Income Tax Assessment Act 1997*

This 3rd gift of papers completes NFSA holdings of material related to Mr Yeldham's career and in total reflects his notable contribution to Australian film and television over past 40 years.

The collection has been very well organised by Mr Yeldham and as a result will facilitate cataloguing by the Archive and ultimately expedient access to the public.

Mr Yeldham's personal memoirs that accompany the collection provide excellent context to the collection as a whole, giving a rare insight into the mind and working methodology of a scriptwriter.

Peter Yeldham has received numerous industry awards and other civic honours including an Order of Australia medal and a Centenary Medal for his contribution and achievements in writing, film and television. NFSA considers this collection of great historical value and worthy of future preservation in the National Collection.

The Department of Communications, Information Technology and the Arts occasionally likes to publicise significant gifts, for example, in its media releases. The identity of the donor would not be divulged unless the donor wished to be named. An image of a work would not be reproduced without permission from the copyright owner.

Do you give permission for DCITA to publicise this gift? Yes ☐ No ☐

Name of authorised officer: GRAHAM SHIRLEY

Position: SENIOR CURATOR, DOCUMENTS & ARTEFACTS, NFSA

Signature: [signed]

Date: 7 / 2 / 2006

August 2003

Statement of Significance of Peter's papers under the Cultural Gifts Program.

Statement on significance of gift to the

National Film and Sound Archive

This collection relates primarily to Australian feature films and television productions and covers the period 1989-1996. It adds to Peter Yeldham's previous donation to the Archive of material relating to his earlier career which covered the period 1950 to 1989.

The collection is very well organised, facilitating accessioning by the Archive, and Peter Yeldham's notes (list of contents and a personal memoir after fifty years as a writer) provide an excellent context for the collection as a whole. The notes will be included as part of the collection as they provide good insight into the life of a scriptwriter.

The material updates the Archive's contemporary television script collection and provides additional depth to coverage of major Australian scriptwriters. It also contains good insight into the scriptwriting process and is useful for researchers in a number of fields including the Australian television and film industry, drama and cultural history.

RI Brent
Director

18 February 1998

Head Office McCoy Circuit Acton ACT • GPO Box 2002 Canberra ACT 2601 • Telephone 06 209 3111 • Facsimile 06 209 3165
Melbourne Office 223 Park Street South Melbourne VIC 3205 • Telephone 03 690 1400 • Facsimile 03 699 4874
Sydney Office 84 Alexander Street Crows Nest NSW 2065 • Telephone 02 438 1477 • Facsimile 02 436 4178

4 February 1999

Legal & Copyright
ABC Ultimo Centre
700 Harris Street
Ultimo NSW 2007
GPO Box 9994
Sydney NSW 2001
DX 601 Sydney
Tel: (02) 9333 5849
Fax: (02) 9333 5860
Email: legal@your.abc.net.au

Mr. PETER YELDHAM
1102 Yarramalong Road
YARRAMALONG NSW 2259

Dear Mr. Yeldham

RE: CAPTAIN JAMES COOK

Further to your correspondence of 25th November 1998 to Mark Slattery, of our international sales department, with regard to the script of the Revcom/ ABC co-produced TV series: 'CAPTAIN JAMES COOK'.

My sincere apologies for the delay in replying to your request to clarify those rights granted in the script agreement of April 1985, between Resolution Films (on behalf of Peter Yeldham) and Revcom, and the rights granted to the ABC in the Revcom/ ABC co-production agreement of December 1986. On assessing all available relevant material, I have now a clarified the ABC's position.

Revcom granted the ABC the right to distribute home videos in Australia and South East Asia on clearance and payment, by the ABC, "of all necessary fees and residuals due to performers, musicians, composers and others who are or may be entitled to any payment for such exploitation." Unfortunately, as the Script Agreement was made between Revcom and Resolution Films, and the ABC appears not to have held a copy of that agreement on file prior to your supplying a copy to Mark Slattery, the assessment of the clearances necessary to distribute home videos by the ABC neglected to include negotiation for the script rights as an ABC responsibility. We regret this oversight.

Given the nature of negotiations and the initial script agreement being outside the Australian Writers Guild Award, the ABC would like to offer a residual payment of 10% of Net Receipts for the Australian/ South East Asia Home Video rights. If this is acceptable we would be pleased to have your formal approval by signature and return of the original of this letter. The copy is for your records.

Should you wish to discuss this matter please do not hesitate to call myself, on (02) 9333 5441, or Wendy Hallam, Manager ABC International, on (02) 9950 3177.

We look forward to your earliest reply.

Kind Regards

ALI EDWARDS
Copyright Officer

I Concur .... Date 5 Feb 1999

Correspondence from the ABC on Captain James Cook.

THE DATE OF THIS AGREEMENT is 27 of March 19 86

THE PARTIES are:

1. REVCOM TELEVISION ~~SAS SPP~~ whose registered office is situated at 1 Rue Taitbout 75009 Paris, France (hereinafter "the Production Company")

2. RESOLUTION FILMS PTY LTD whose registered office is situated at 2 Florence St., Cremorne. 2090....... NEW SOUTH WALES (hereinafter "the Development Company")

3. PETER YELDHAM PRODUCTIONS PTY LTD whose registered office is situated at 20 LAVONI ST MOSMAN, NEW SOUTH WALES (hereinafter "the Writing Company")

4. PETER YELDHAM of 20 LAVONI ST MOSMAN, NEW SOUTH WALES (hereinafter "the Associate Producer")

5. GEOFFREY DANIELS of 3/14 AVENUE RD MOSMAN, NEW SOUTH WALES (hereinafter "the Executive Producer")

RECITALS:

A. Peter Yeldham is the author of an original literary and dramatic work entitled "The Wind and the Stars" being a screenplay dramatising the life of Captain Cook (hereinafter "the Work").

B. The Development Company owns an exclusive option over the world television and allied rights in the Work throughout the world free from encumbrances for the legal term of copyright including the right to license or assign the said rights.

C. The Production Company is desirous of acquiring world television rights in the Work in order to produce a television mini-series for exploitation throughout the world (hereinafter "the Series").

D. The Development Company agrees to grant the Production Company world television rights on the terms and for the consideration set out herein. All subsidiary and allied

Agreement between Revcom, Resolution, Peter's company and the producers, Peter and Geoff Daniels.

16 December 2011

ABC
Australian
Broadcasting
Corporation

Peter Yeldham OAM
214 Yarramalong Road
Wyong Creek
Yarramalong Valley 2259

ABC Ultimo Centre
700 Harris Street
Ultimo NSW 2007

GPO Box 9994
Sydney NSW 2001

Tel. +61 2 8333 1500
abc.net.au

Dear Mr Yeldham

Thank you for your letter of 0 December to the Managing Director, which Mr Scott has asked me to respond to on his behalf.

Regrettably the Managing Director's office has no record of your letter of 20 September nor the email enclosed with the letter. In any case, I have sought comments from the ABC's commercial arm in light of the concerns raised in your most recent correspondence and they advise me that the ABC has never had the video rights to *Captain James Cook*.

I understand that ABC Video as it was then know attempted to secure the video rights in 1987 but was unsuccessful and the original video rights were licensed by Revcom to Reel Corporation. Reel Corporation also acquired the DVD rights for Australia in 2002, however the DVD was deleted from the Reel catalogue when the rights expired in approximately 2007 or 2008. If you require further information regarding the commercial retail distribution of *Captain James Cook* I would recommend you contact Reel DVD. Their postal address is GPO 2581, Sydney, 2009 and they also have a customer service enquiry line on 1300 657 780.

I am sorry I do not have better news for you but can assure you that the ABC has the utmost respect for the work you have produced in conjunction with the ABC and for the outstanding contribution you have made to the film and television industries both in Australia and overseas.

Yours sincerely

Kirstin McLiesh
Head, ABC Audience and Consumer Affairs

Part Thirteen: Emails, Diaries, Letters and Selected Works

Penguin Group (Australia)
250 Camberwell Road, Camberwell, VIC 3124
Telephone +61 (3) 9811 2400
Fax +61 (3) 9811 2620
www.penguin.com.au

19 December 2005

Peter Yeldham
1102 Yarramalong Rd
Yarramalong NSW 2259

Dear Peter,

I'm delighted to enclose two advance copies of your wonderful novel, *The Murrumbidgee Kid*. We hope you are as pleased as we are with the finished product. We all think it looks just beautiful – and feels it too. Very chunky and nice to hold! Congratulations. We feel sure that this is the first of many Peter Yeldham/Penguin novels.

For your records, the official publication date is 6 February 2005 and the recommended retail price is $29.95. Our target sales for this print run are 10,000 copies. You will receive your remaining author copies shortly directly from the warehouse, and if you'd like to purchase more at our author discount rate please contact Julia Moffitt on 03 9811 2578 or email julia.moffitt@au.penguingroup.com. The other good news is that as a Penguin author, you can purchase all Penguin books at a discount.

Congratulations once more, Peter, and I am looking forward to working with you again in the not-too-distant future. You were what us editors call 'a dream author': patient, helpful, receptive…a rare find!

Warm regards,

Saskia

Saskia Adams
Editor – Books for Adults

A PEARSON COMPANY

A DIVISION OF PEARSON AUSTRALIA GROUP PTY LTD ABN 40 004 245 943 250 CAMBERWELL ROAD, CAMBERWELL, VIC 3124

Saskia Adams, from Penguin, writes to Peter on the publication of The Murumbidgee Kid.

SELECTED WORKS

Novels
Above the Fold. 2014.
Against the Tide. 1999.
Barbed Wire and Roses. 2007.
A Bitter Harvest. 1997.
The Currency Lads. 1998.
A Distant Shore. 2009.
Dragons in the Forest. 2015.
Glory Girl. 2010.
Land of Dreams. 2002.
The Last Double Sunrise. 2017.
The Murrumbidgee Kid. 2006.
Reprisal. 1994.
Two Sides of a Triangle. 1996.
Without Warning. 1995.

Stage Plays
Birds on the Wing. 1969.
But She Won't Lie Down: A Comedy Thriller in Two Acts. 1978.
Fringe Benefits: A Comedy. Written with Donald Churchill. 1976.
Lighting Up Time: A Comedy. Written with Martin Worth. 1984.
My Friend Miss Flint: A Comedy. Written with Donald Churchill.
Seven Little Australians. With John Palmer and Jim Graham. Music by David Reeves. 1988.
Split Down the Middle. 1998.

Film Screenplays
The Age of Consent. 1969.
Boundaries of the Heart. 1988.
The Comedy Man. 1964.
The Liquidator. 1965.
The Long Duel. 1967.
Mozambique. 1965.
Our Man in Marrakesh. 1966.
Ten Little Indians. 1965.

Television Miniseries
1915. 1981.
The Alien Years. 1988.
The Battlers. 1994.
Birds on the Wing. 1971.
Captain James Cook. 1987.
The Far Country. 1987.
Flight Into Hell. 1985.
Golden Soak. 1979.
Harriet's Back In Town. 1972-.
The Heroes. 1988.
Heroes II: The Return. 1992.
Jessica. 2004.
The Lancaster-Miller Affair. 1997.
The Levkas Man. 1981.
Naked Under Capricorn. 1989.
The Private War of Lucinda Smith. 1990
Ride on Stranger. 1979.
Run from the Morning. 1978.
Sporting Chance. 1981.
The Timeless Land. 1980.
Tusitala. 1986.

Television plays
The Cabbage Tree Hat Boys. 1965.
The Hostages. 1997.
The Juggler. 1970.
Money in the Bank. 1979.
A Really Good Jazz Piano. 1964.
Reprisal. 1997.
Reunion Day. 1962.
Thunder on the Snowy. 1960.
Touch and Go. 1979.
Weekend of Shadows. 1977.
Without Warning. 1999.

www.ingramcontent.com/pod-product-compliance
Lightning Source LLC
Chambersburg PA
CBHW051535010526
44107CB00064B/2739